P9-BYY-997

Sharon
OSBOURNE

BY THE SAME AUTHOR:

Ozzy Unauthorized

Rags to Richie (by Shane Richie,
with Sue Crawford)

Sharon
OSBOURNE

UNAUTHORIZED, UNCENSORED – UNDERSTOOD

SUE CRAWFORD

MICHAEL O'MARA BOOKS LIMITED

First published in 2005 by
Michael O'Mara Books Limited
9 Lion Yard, Tremadoc Road
London sw4 7nq

Copyright © Sue Crawford 2005

The right of Sue Crawford to be identified as the author
of this work has been asserted by her in accordance with the
Copyright, Designs and Patents Act 1988.

All rights reserved. No part of this publication may be
reproduced, stored in a retrieval system, or transmitted by any
means, without the prior permission in writing of the publisher,
nor be otherwise circulated in any form of binding or cover
other than that in which it is published and without a similar
condition including this condition being imposed on the
subsequent purchaser.

A CIP catalogue record for this book is available
from the British Library.

ISBN 1-84317-148-1

1 3 5 7 9 10 8 6 4 2

www.mombooks.com

Designed and typeset by Martin Bristow

Printed and bound in England by Clays Ltd, St Ives plc

Contents

Author's Acknowledgements

Thanks to the many people who helped with the compilation of this biography. In no particular order these include Eileen Somers for her wonderful memory and amusing anecdotes about family life, Anne Sheward for her fond recollections of Sharon's childhood and Rick Sky and Ken Lennox for their insights into life on the road with Sharon and Ozzy. Countless others generously gave their time and shared their memories, but would prefer to remain anonymous; their help was also much appreciated.

At Michael O'Mara Books I would like to thank Michael O'Mara for commissioning the book, Editorial Director Toby Buchan and Editor Kate Gribble for their enthusiasm, guidance and support and Judith Palmer for the amazing picture selection. Thanks also to Emily Gale for her sensitive and thorough copy-editing. I am particularly grateful to Sarah Jones for her tireless and painstaking research, which made my job so much easier.

A thank you must also go to Chris Watson and his team at Ibas UK for retrieving Chapters Two to Four from computer netherworld.

And finally, thank you to Sharon Osbourne for generously revealing the frank details of her extraordinary life 'because I've got such a big mouth,' and for being such a fascinating and endearing great British eccentric who roused my curiosity enough to write this book.

There is a Chinese curse that says, 'May you live in interesting times.' Sharon has done just that, yet she has handled everything life has thrown at her with courage, humility and humour, proving an inspiration to us all.

SUE CRAWFORD
February 2005

SOURCES

Researching this book has been a mammoth task, involving numerous newspapers, magazines, one-to-one interviews, websites, books, television programmes and DVDs. The books written by Sharon's father, Don Arden (*Mr Big*), and the Osbournes themselves (*Ordinary People*) proved rich sources of inspiration and anecdote. As well as these, I am indebted to the following publications and television programmes: the *Daily Express*, the *Daily Mail*, the *Guardian*, the *Sun*, the *Independent*, the *Daily Star*, the *Sunday Mirror*, the *Sunday Times*, the *Mail on Sunday*, the *News of the World*, the *New York Daily News*, the *City News Service*, *Q* magazine, *People* magazine, *Kerrang!* magazine, *Melody Maker*, *Rolling Stone*, *Entertainment Weekly*, *Good Morning America* (ABC), *Parkinson* (ITV), *Larry King Live* (CNN), *Crimewatch* (BBC), and Barbara Walters's interview (ABC News 20/20, 6 November 2002). For books and DVDs, please see page 217.

Photograph Acknowledgements

Page 1: Eileen Somers (*above*), Scopefeatures.com (*below*)

Page 2: © Neal Preston/Corbis (*above & centre*), © Neal Preston/Retna Ltd (*below*)

Page 3: © Neal Preston/Retna Ltd (*above*), George Chin/WireImage.com (*below*)

Page 4: © Neal Preston/Corbis (above), Eddie Sanderson/Scopefeatures.com (*below*)

Page 5: Richard Young/Rex Features (*above*), © Dave Morgan/Alpha (*below*)

Page 6: © Tom Wagner/Corbis (*above*), © Neal Preston/Corbis (*below*)

Page 7: © Reuters/Corbis (*both*)

Page 8: © Ron Sachs/Corbis

Page 9: Jon Furniss/WireImage.com

Page 10: © Neal Preston/Corbis (*above*), Eileen Somers (*below*)

Page 11: Stewart Cook/Rex Features (*above*), © Michael Kitada/Orange County Register/Corbis (*below*)

Page 12: © Fred Prouser/Reuters/Corbis (*above*), © Dave Parker/Alpha (*below*)

Page 13: Rex Features (*above*), © Darla Khazei/Retna Ltd (*below left*), Alex Berliner/BEI/Rex Features (*below right*)

Page 14: Rex Features (*above left & right*), Ray Tang/Rex Features (*below*)

Page 15: Richard Young/Rex Features (*above*), Ian West/ PA/Empics (*below*)

Page 16: © Reuters/Corbis (*above*), Gregg DeGuire/ WireImage.com (*below*)

Foreword
Sharon Rachel Osbourne

❝ *My husband is a drug addict and an alcoholic
and he tried to kill me. Me? I am a spendaholic.
What more is there to know?* ❞

WHEN SHARON OSBOURNE booked herself into hospital for a gastric banding operation in 1999, she could have had no idea the impact that simple decision would have on her entire life. A devoted mother and wife and manager to legendary rocker Ozzy Osbourne, Sharon had always put other people first, neglecting both her appearance and her dreams.

Yet that operation proved to be the start of a remarkable reinvention which, six years later, would see her transformed into a global brand with a profile so high it almost eclipses that of her husband. With newly whitened teeth, neatly coiffured hair and a figure and face the envy of Hollywood, she has emerged from the shadows, carving out her own unique niche and establishing herself as a strong, confident and forthright woman, capable of tackling anything and anyone.

By her own admission a late bloomer, she has inspired millions of women, embracing both her life and her age. 'My attitude is that if I can do this, that's good because it empowers other women,' she says simply. And certainly at the moment she can do no wrong. Now a razor-tongued judge on *The X Factor*, a chat-show favourite, the new face of Asda supermarkets, the star of a West End show, the world-famous mum in television's most eccentric family show *The Osbournes*, and a successful rock manager and entrepreneur, there seems no end to her talents.

Yet incredibly, without that dramatic weight loss – Sharon lost nearly eight stone, almost halving her body weight – it is unlikely that anyone outside the closed world of rock music would have known anything about her. As she admits: 'I couldn't have put myself up there if I'd been the old Sharon. The old Sharon hid herself behind fat. When I realized that, I had to do something about it.'

The weight loss gave her the public profile she had secretly yearned for and a lifestyle most people only dream of. Yet even during those years outside the public eye Sharon crammed in more than many people do in an entire lifetime. The daughter of music promoter Don Arden, she had an unorthodox childhood where work took precedence over family life, and birthdays and Christmas were rarely celebrated. In the late 1960s she became a party-loving teenager with a taste for drink and the high life. Yet, even then, her appetite for fun was juxtaposed with an intense desire to succeed, as she carved out a successful career as a tour manager to some of rock's biggest names.

When she rescued Ozzy from the gutter in 1979 she was credited with saving both his career and his life, but at the same time she acknowledged that he too had saved her. Without him she believes she would have ended up an uncompromising and even intimidating businesswoman whose work meant everything. 'In other words, doing business the way my father did.'

They married, but 'happy ever after' was never part of the equation. Miscarriages, a bitter twenty-year feud with her father and drink- and drug-fuelled years on the road with Ozzy and three young children in tow, made for an eventful life. Yet this only told part of the story. For at home Sharon was no different to countless working mums the world over. Devoted to her children, worrying about their schooling and childcare, she fought to give them the best possible start in life, while at the same time struggling to hold down a career in the notoriously male-orientated rock business, which for years dismissed her as 'the fat wife'.

Since then there has been Ozzy's attempt to strangle her, her brave battle with colon cancer and the drugs problems of two of her children, Kelly and Jack. Yet through it all she has guided her family to international superstardom and grossed a multi-million-pound fortune along the way.

Today, at fifty-two, Sharon remains a woman of immense contradictions. A shopaholic who will spend thousands on clothes without batting an eyelid, yet at the same time a devoted and generous supporter of charities, including the Tsunami Appeal. Soft-hearted – when *The X Factor*'s vulnerable youngsters cried as their chance of fame was snatched away, the tears she wept were real; but make no mistake – she is nobody's fool. Promoters and musicians who have crossed her over the years still tremble as they recount her verbal and physical onslaughts. Explains Sharon: 'I have the vocabulary of a truck driver. There's a mean motherfucker behind this smile.'

She is glamorous and intelligent, yet foul-mouthed and entirely unconventional – *The Osbournes* (her brainchild) brought her unique style of mothering to the nation's attention. Yet her hopes and her dreams and, in many ways, her lifestyle, are no different to those of women everywhere. Her family come first: her children, her husband, her dogs and her home.

Little wonder that a 2004 survey by the Mothers' Union found that 12 per cent of women felt she was a good role model for other mothers. The Anglican charity is dedicated to promoting marriage and family life and has a somewhat old-fashioned image, but somehow Sharon was capable of striking a chord with its members.

One of the most complex and compelling women to emerge on to the public stage for years, she has a simple philosophy: 'I don't want to be the richest person in the graveyard. I don't want to regret anything. I don't want to wait. I want to taste it, live it, fuck it, eat it all now.' It means that there is little she hasn't already achieved in her life, yet a great deal more she wants to do: today she has a career ahead of her that women half her age could only wish for.

As Sharon says with her typical trademark honesty: 'My life has been like a Jackie Collins novel. Sometimes I sit down and think "Jesus Christ, what a ride."' What lies ahead no one knows, but one thing is for sure, Sharon holds all the cards, and if the future turns out to be only half as thrilling as the past, it will continue to be an amazing journey.

CHAPTER ONE

Show Business Born and Bred

*❧ I couldn't sing or dance and I had no talent.
I must have auditioned for* The Sound of Music
twenty fucking times. ❧

THE LITTLE GIRL SCREAMED until she was red in the face before dramatically throwing herself to the floor with tears streaming down her cheeks. 'She hit me, Daddy! She's evil! Please don't send me back there! No, no, no, Daddy!' To an outsider the scene might have resembled something from Dickensian times: a small, terrified child begging her father not to send her back to the school where she was being so brutally treated.

It would take a father with a heart of stone not to be moved by such pitiful pleadings and Don Arden, for all his uncompromising business dealings, was as soft-hearted as the next daddy when it came to his family. Devoted to his pretty young daughter Sharon and enraged by her allegations of ill treatment, he vowed to put an instant end to her suffering. The next day he bundled Sharon into the passenger seat of his Rolls-Royce and drove to the school gates, determined to have it out with the teacher who had dared raise a finger to his precious girl.

But when he was shown through to the staff room to confront the woman in question, Don's jaw dropped in shock and disbelief. For the woman standing there in front of him was not some sinister-looking monster fiercely waving a large cane, but a sweet, frail old lady, with a beatific smile and the air of a living saint, dressed in a tweed skirt and carrying a walking stick. Recalled Don: 'She must have been ninety if she was a day. And that was when I realized I'd fallen for one of Sharon's fairy stories again. One thing about my daughter, she has never lacked persistence – or imagination.' In years to come, such capacity for drama and invention would be the very characteristics that would turn Sharon into an international star, in the hilarious MTV fly-on-the-wall documentary series *The Osbournes* and on ITV's hit music show *The X Factor*. But back then such histrionics were merely the hallmark of a quick-witted young girl, who clearly loved theatre – as did the family she was born into.

Sharon's father Don was born Harry Levy, in Manchester, 1926. It was a poor Jewish household, but his mother Sarah, known to her friends as Sally, was passionate about the theatre and would take Harry and his older sister Eileen whenever they could afford it. By the time he was nine Harry and his mother were already planning how he would be a big star someday. With nowhere else to practice, Harry would stand out in the street singing and doing impressions, much to the amusement of the neighbours and his friends.

As soon as he got the chance, following a brief spell in the army, Harry moved to London and changed his name to Don Arden. He never looked back. Variety was just taking off in the capital and Don, who by now had developed his own variety act, soon found himself earning £350 a show – a fortune back in the late 1940s.

In 1949 Don met and fell in love with a glamorous former dancer by the name of Hope Shaw. Everyone called her 'Paddles' – a nickname that had stuck from her pre-war years when she had worked as an acrobatic dancer under the stage name of Paddy O'Shea. A stunning blonde, she ran a large house in Brixton, south London, that doubled as showbiz digs for travelling entertainers. Top British comedy double act Morecambe and Wise were regular guests, as was comedian Tommy Cooper. At an after-show theatre party one evening Hope was introduced to Don. Seven years older than him and with two children from a previous marriage – Richard and Dixie – she was an unlikely conquest for the cocksure young entertainer, but Don was immediately smitten. Confident and intelligent, there was a depth to her he'd never found in girls his own age. What's more she shared his show-business dreams and on 21 April 1950 they were married at Lambeth Register Office, with Richard and Dixie taking Don's surname.

As fans of the TV series *The Osbournes* know, family feuds and fights are legendary in the Osbourne household and, ironically, Sharon was caught up in one such drama before she was even born. With Hope already a mother of two, plus the large age gap between them, Don reckoned his strict Jewish mother would not approve of the marriage. Rather than face her wrath he took the easy way out and kept it quiet. It was only when their first child, David, was born on 6 February 1951 that Don finally broke the news about his new family. Predictably his mother was furious and refused even to meet Hope or her new grandson. It wasn't until the birth of Sharon on 9 October 1952 that Sally Levy finally came round.

Sharon Rachel Arden was born at Westminster Hospital, right in the centre of London. After an overnight stay her proud parents took her back to the family home at 68 Angell Road, Brixton. By now Don had earned enough money to lease a huge Victorian mansion, with four floors and seven bedrooms. The top three flights were the family home where Don, Hope and the four children lived, and the ground floor he converted into his offices. The house belonged to Winifred Atwell, the black pianist, who had specifically snapped up property in the area to rent out to other performers. Although Brixton today is best known as a cosmopolitan area and in the 1980s developed a reputation for crime following serious race riots, in the 1950s it was an area famous as a colourful community for artists and entertainers. With so many bedrooms in the house Hope occasionally fell back into her old business, renting out rooms to old show-business friends when they were playing in town. It was a happy and carefree scene, if a little chaotic, and Don revelled in it, vowing to travel less and take on more work in London now he had a young family.

One of the very first visitors to Brixton to meet the newborn Sharon was her Aunty Eileen. Don had remained close to his family in Manchester since moving to London. He was devoted to his mother Sally and would see her as frequently as his busy touring schedule allowed, taking her expensive gifts on every visit. His sister Eileen and her husband Harry Somers lived just around the corner from his mother and, typically of older sisters, Eileen was one of Don's fiercest and proudest admirers. Having missed out on celebrating the birth of David, she wasn't going to be cheated a second time and when Sharon was born Eileen jumped straight onto a train and headed for the capital, armed with handmade baby clothes to spoil her new niece. Whenever Don was appearing in shows in the north of England he would take his family with him and stay at his mother's house. A delighted Eileen relished the opportunity to get to know her nephew and niece better and even knitted two little coats for them – beige for Sharon and dark red for David.

In 1955, when Sharon was three, Don was hired as a special guest for a twenty-week run of *The Black and White Minstrel Show* – an old vaudeville-style BBC Television show, in which the male singers and dancers were required to 'black up' to play their parts. The show was hugely popular at the time – the mainstay of the BBC's Saturday-night schedule – and it exposed Don's variety act to a whole new audience. Yet despite his success on the stage Don was restless. Increasingly he was growing convinced that variety had had its day. Having kept a sharp eye on the latest trends in America, he knew that television and rock-and-roll music were on the way in and sensed that his fortune lay elsewhere – perhaps on the other side of the fence. Eventually he made his decision: rather than appear on stage, he would now organize events – booking artists and producing shows. It was a bold move and one that would also entail a huge change of lifestyle. To ensure a show ran smoothly Don physically needed to be there. Not only in Britain, but also throughout Europe. He had cottoned on to the fact that tens of thousands of bored US troops were stationed all over Europe, particularly in Germany. They couldn't easily get to shows, so he would take the shows to them. He needed Hope's help for such a mammoth task. Richard and Dixie were now in their late teens and able to fend for themselves, but Sharon and David, he decided, would travel with them.

The effect on family life was dramatic, as Sharon recalled: 'I spent the first five years of my life going from one military base to another. They'd leave us in the hotel while they did the show and then come back and get us. Nobody would do it today. You'd get arrested.' A more sensitive child would understandably have been frightened or, at the very least, a little unsettled at being left alone night after night in strange hotels, in a strange country. But not Sharon. A confident and mischievous child, as soon as her parents were out of the door for the evening show,

Sharon would throw back the bed sheets and shake her brother awake. The two of them would sneak out of their room and head straight for the elevators, racing each other up and down, screaming with laughter as the night porter tried in vain to catch them. The more he shouted at them in German, the more they would laugh, not understanding a single word of his rage. When they tired of that particular game they would break into the kitchens in the dead of night after the staff had gone to bed, roaming wild like a couple of feral cats. Even at the age of five, Sharon could not be tamed.

Not surprisingly such an unorthodox start in life gave Sharon a lifelong disregard for authority and routine. Sensing this rebellious streak in her, when Sharon reached school age Don decided to do something about it. Like any father he wanted only the best for his daughter and insisted on putting Sharon into a top private school. It cost him a fortune, but the expense made no difference – even at this early age Sharon had little interest in academic life and would simply fool around in the lessons, refusing to pay attention, idling away the hours until the bell rang.

By now Don had moved on to organizing the European tours of the most celebrated American musicians of the time. Such was his close working relationship with them that when they were in London many of them would stay with him and Hope. To keep his empire running smoothly Don was now working every hour God sent – home and office life had begun to blur into one. Many an evening would begin with Don taking international phone calls in one room and Hope cooking up dinner for Sam Cooke or Bill Haley and the Comets in another. Sharon's earliest memories were not of teddy bears and cuddles with her mother, but being backstage and meeting names such as Little Richard, Jerry Lee Lewis, Gene Vincent, Brenda Lee and the Everly Brothers. She says: 'I can remember being at Victoria Station at midnight, putting Bill Haley on a train to Europe, when I was five, because my Dad had him over from America to do a European tour. And then after that, it was Sam Cooke. I fell madly in love with Sam Cooke at age seven. He used to wear these high-cut matador trousers, and he was built a little bit like Prince, so he had a really neat little body. His cologne was so gorgeous that I could smell where he'd been backstage, and I can remember cowering when he'd come out.' It was Gene Vincent, meanwhile, who taught her to swim: 'His withered leg used to dangle in the water.'

But as exciting as life undoubtedly was, there was a downside to it too. Don and Hope were so wrapped up in work that the usual traditions of family life often went by the wayside. Christmas was not a big event; Sharon and David did not have birthday parties and were never encouraged to bring their friends home for tea. Sharon didn't have a favourite doll because she didn't have any dolls. As she later explained: 'I hate to use the word normal, because I don't think it exists, but we didn't have a normal upbringing. There were never birthday parties or Christmas parties as our social life all revolved around work. It was a great way to be brought up, but it was strange.' Don was preoccupied with his job and never gave the minutiae of family life much thought. Hope's life revolved around Don. She was devoted to him – his needs came first – and although she loved her children she was not particularly maternal.

Don had developed a reputation as a heavy-handed businessman who, by his own admission, ruled by fear. He wasn't afraid to use threats and intimidation – and even physical methods – to get his own way if he felt he was being double-crossed. There was Don's way of doing business and there was no other way. Cross him and you'd probably live to regret it. According to Sharon: 'My dad was always threatening people. I was never allowed to bring friends home. It was always business. We didn't know anyone who didn't perform or write or produce. I used to go and stay with my school friend and I couldn't believe the way she lived, how normal it was. Then I'd go back to my house where everything was knocked off and there would be gangsters or some guy running around with a gun. I was surrounded by a lot of violence as a child, a lot of crime. I mean my father was a two-bit hood.'

With such drama going on at home, not surprisingly Sharon was paying even less attention in lessons. The travelling she had done as a young child had ruined her as far as school was concerned and she could never settle down enough to study. When she grew tired of a particular school, which she always did, she would simply come home and regale her father with terrible tales of how she had been ill-treated. Claiming she had been brutalized by the frail old lady was her *pièce de résistance*, but there were countless other dramas along the way. And Don, the toughest of businessmen who would stand no nonsense in the world of work, was putty in his daughter's hands. What's more, Sharon knew it.

At school, back in London, Sharon's confidence and sense of humour made her popular in the playground, but the combination of her fleeting stays at schools and her unorthodox home life meant she rarely had the opportunity to make long-lasting friends. Instead she spent her time with David, playing truant, going to the cinema or to the local Woolworths where they would dare each other to misbehave. Not that Sharon was upset by her lack of close friends or ever felt intimidated. She may have stood out from the crowd, but there was no way she would ever be bullied for it.

For her ninth birthday Don had proudly bought her a Star of David necklace and matching earrings to celebrate her Jewish roots. His heritage was important to him and he wanted Sharon to feel the same way. Delighted by his generosity, Sharon was eager to show off her first expensive jewels and proudly wore them to school the following day. But that afternoon, as she and David took a shortcut home down an alley, they were stopped by a group of children who saw the necklace and began yelling racial abuse at them. The scene grew uglier and uglier and the boys grew louder and louder, egging each other on with every shout. As they started to circle David, it soon became clear that the terrified little boy was not going to escape the gang without a serious beating and that Sharon would lose her jewels. As David looked around in desperation, every escape route sealed off, he suddenly heard an ear-piercing scream. Sharon. It was enough to stop the gang in their tracks. As they turned round she squared up to them, half their size, spitting and yelling abuse twice as loud and three times as offensive. She may have been a few years younger than the gang and she was certainly outnumbered, but Sharon didn't know the meaning of the word fear. Shocked, they backed off and a triumphant Sharon returned home giggling with delight. Just as she would relish every spat with Simon Cowell in years to come, Sharon was totally unfazed by the confrontation, revelling in her victory. 'Even then I had a mouth,' she later recalled.

Whenever Don could get a rare break from his work he would travel back to Manchester, taking Hope, Sharon and David with him. His mother Sally now had a nice semi-detached house in a middle-class suburb and Sharon adored staying with her – it was a taste of ordinary family life that she never experienced at home and she lapped it up. Her grandmother would take her on the bus into the centre of Manchester and make a fuss of her in the way that only grandmothers do. After a trip around the shops and department stores Sharon would be taken to one of the city's finest hotels, where her grandmother would teach her to sit nicely and speak like a lady as they enjoyed a smart lunch. It was the sort of thing she rarely did with her mother and Sharon relished every second of it, proudly copying her grandmother's old-fashioned manners. Sharon and David also got on well with their Aunty Eileen's two children, Cathy and Danny. Danny was the same age as Sharon and Cathy was eight years younger, and the four children would enjoy hours of fun playing in Eileen's back garden.

On other occasions Danny would travel to London with his grandmother to stay with Don and Hope. It was during one of these trips that Sharon developed her lifelong love of dogs. Sally Levy loved animals and whenever she took Sharon and Danny out for the day, she would walk them past the pet shop and point out the cutest dogs in the window. Not surprisingly both Sharon and Danny later pleaded with their parents to be allowed a pet of their own. But while Danny's mum Eileen refused, due to a lifelong fear of dogs, Sharon succeeded in winding Don around her little finger and was soon the proud owner of two dogs. They were allowed to rule the roost and Sharon lavished them with attention and affection. The only time they were banished outside was during Aunty Eileen's visits, to avoid frightening her. Even then Sharon could not bear to be parted from the dogs for long. Eileen recalls: 'The family had double-glazed patio windows before anyone had even heard of double-glazing and I remember Sharon pressing her nose up against the windows, looking outside and saying sadly: "The dogs will have to stay outside while you're here." She was very devoted to them.'

By now Don had invested some of his money in a summer holiday home. It was a simple ground-floor flat, but it was right by the beach at Minnis Bay, near Margate in Kent. Whenever he could he would drive out there for the weekend with the family, often inviting his mother down from Manchester to stay with them. But as close as Sharon was to her father's family, the geographical distance between them gradually began to prove more and more of a hurdle. With Don's life revolving almost entirely around work, it was his friends and business associates that the family would stay with at weekends and during their travels around the country. It wasn't long before Sharon was referring to them as her aunties and uncles, in addition to her Aunty Eileen and Uncle Harry.

As a young girl Sharon had dreamed of becoming a ballerina. While those childish fantasies had more or less disappeared by the time she was eleven, she was still set on a life in show business. How much of this was her wish to escape from academic lessons and how much a genuine desire to appear on stage is unclear, but in 1963 Sharon finally had her way after months of nagging, having persuaded her father that she would be better off being educated at the Italia Conti stage school. Founded in 1911 by the actress Italia Conti, the school was renowned for giving youngsters the best possible preparation and training for the professional stage and screen. Based in Landor Road in Clapham, south London, it was not far from the Arden family household. Still, had the journey to school involved a four-hour daily commute it is unlikely Don would have been able to stand in Sharon's way.

Sharon's brother David was already a pupil at the school, yet rather than pave the way for Sharon his presence simply created problems. A blond, blue-eyed, good-looking boy, David was popular with teachers and other pupils alike. He was the school heart-throb and when Sharon arrived she found him a hard act to follow. Like many brothers and sisters they fought like cat and dog at home and with the school being such a small one they found the closed environment merely added to the pressures. In despair, hearing daily reports of their continuing squabbles, Don withdrew Sharon and placed her in a private school near by.

Don meanwhile was as busy as ever, flitting backwards and forwards between Britain and the States, picking up on the latest acts. He even succeeded in persuading Hollywood sex symbol Jayne Mansfield to come over to Britain to appear in a London show. Sharon was around twelve at the time and pleaded to be allowed to go along to meet this living legend. Worried that the material might not be suitable for a young girl, Don insisted that after the introductions Sharon and Hope would wait in Jayne's dressing room while the show took place. Many young girls would have sat in a corner and sulked at such treatment, but not Sharon. For a young girl obsessed with the bright lights, it was an opportunity too good to miss. And while her mother sat in a corner idly flicking through magazines Sharon danced around the room, trying on every item in Jayne's glamorous wardrobe, from thigh-high white leather boots to padded bras.

When Sharon reached the age of thirteen, and with David about to leave, Don finally gave in to her relentless pestering and allowed her to return to the Italia Conti. Respected actress Olivia Hussey was a contemporary of Sharon's, as was Italia Conti's current principal Anne Sheward, who became one of her best friends during her time there. The two were in many of the same classes, including ballet, dance and elocution. Anne remembers Sharon as a charismatic and quick-witted girl who was always one step ahead of the rest of the class.

On Monday mornings the pupils would return from their weekend full of dread for their hated elocution lessons. When it came to her turn to recite to the class, without fail Sharon would stand up, smile sweetly and apologize, telling the teacher that the reason she hadn't learnt her lines was that she had broken her glasses. The teacher was a particularly forgetful one and the following week, totally unabashed, Sharon would stand up in front of the class again with the same story. As Anne Sheward recalls: 'And she'd never worn glasses in her life! You don't mess with Sharon Osbourne. You never did. She always had a tremendously big personality. She had very good manners, but she was a real character, very quick and very shrewd; she was nobody's fool. Yet at the same time she was very kind. If you were a friend of Sharon's she would stick by you through thick and thin. She was warm and very popular. There was no pretence; if she didn't like something about you she'd tell you. What you saw was what you got and people liked that about her.'

Dance, and particularly ballet, was still Sharon's favourite subject at school. While she was smaller than the other dancers her natural talent shone through and soon after rejoining the school she succeeded in winning a part in a West End pantomime. The show ran for several weeks and meant that Sharon was unable to travel to Manchester to take part in her cousin Danny's bar mitzvah, much to the disappointment of her relatives. On her next visit to see them, Sharon apologized and proudly handed her Aunty Eileen a framed photograph of herself in her ballet dancer's costume. Eileen was delighted her niece had gone to such effort and for years the picture took pride of place on the cabinet in the front room.

The ballet role had meant a lot to Sharon, who was not finding herself an automatic choice for school productions. She would audition regularly, but time and time again felt she was losing out in favour of the skinny blonde girls that seemed to surround her. Sharon was always immaculately dressed but, like her parents, she was neither tall nor naturally slim and would periodically diet in an attempt to lose a few pounds. As Anne recalls: 'She was always quite hung-up about her weight, even as a child. We were sitting in Leicester Square one day and I was quite skinny at the time and Sharon wasn't and I can remember her saying: "I've only got to look at a chip and I put on two pounds!" She wasn't huge by any means, but she was heavy and certainly didn't have the long limbs of a typical dancer; she was tiny – she was only about five feet.'

By now Sharon was beginning to grow disillusioned. She still had little interest in academic life, lacking the discipline to complete homework on time and concentrate in lessons, and predictably began to find other diversions. She and a group of friends would often meet at the Pancake House in Leicester Square, or the local Wimpy outlet where Sharon would order burger and chips, leaving the bun if she was on one of her frequent diets. There was a pub right next door to the school and as soon as she was old enough to carry it off, she would don make-up and sneak off for lunch, beer and a chat. Recalls Anne: 'She always had a twinkle in her eye and was great fun. She had a good sense of humour and she wasn't slow at coming forward.'

Back at home, business for Don was booming. He was by now the most successful music entrepreneur in the country. He had offices in the West End of London and later that year the family left Brixton and moved to a beautiful old mansion in Mayfair. Don's drive and ambition had taken them far. As he saw it, money was for spending, and the more ostentatious ways he could find to do it the better. The family no longer had one Rolls-Royce, they had three. And if one was scratched Don simply sold it and bought another. He thought nothing of splashing out £10,000 on an impulse buy of an antique table – or spoiling his children. David, who by now was nearly seventeen, was allowed to hold lavish parties for his student friends, to which Sharon and her friends would tag along. For Sharon they were great occasions to dress up in the latest fashions and jewellery – all paid for by her doting father. As she admitted later: 'I had a charmed upbringing.'

But she also maintained that life in the Arden household was a roller coaster, recalling that as well as the ups, there were the downs, too: 'I was the girl who moved from Brixton to Mayfair overnight. He'd go from running a huge empire to bankruptcy and back again. We lived in this huge house, but we had no phone or electricity because we hadn't paid the bills.'

Indeed, Sharon claimed that when things got really bad, the bailiffs would come in and take the furniture and the family's other prized possessions away. But strangely she shed no tears. For many children seeing their home invaded and stripped bare by strangers would have been an unsettling experience, but Sharon simply stood at Don's side and watched as objects were taken out. The reason was simple: she idolized her father and trusted that he would always take care of her. He certainly had a terrifying streak to his nature and would occasionally scream and bawl when the children misbehaved, but in Sharon's world there was nobody quite like him. 'When you are a child and you have someone so strong and so powerful and so successful as your father, you look up to them,' she once explained. 'Everything he did I thought was right – whatever he said, his opinions, his actions. He was my dad. He was my icon.'

Yet as close as Sharon was to her father, she did not share a similar relationship with her mother. She and Don were alike – obstinate, sparky and full of energy and fire – and he had doted on her since the day she was born. But Sharon and her mum were chalk and cheese. Sharon always felt that Hope preferred her brother and, even as a little girl, she always ran straight for her father. As she explained years later: 'It's very hard to admit, but I simply didn't like her. If I ever hurt myself as a child I'd never run to her for a hug to make it better. There was never that bond between us.'

By now Sharon was fifteen and growing increasingly restless with her life. She had realized that her larger size meant she was not going to make it as a professional dancer and that her fortune probably lay on the other side of the fence, as it had for Don. She had joked her way through her years at the Italia Conti, but her headmistress had made it clear she could not see much of a future for her. Sharon agreed; she had simply had enough of formal lessons and academic life. Confident and smart and impatient to make her mark on the world, she begged her father to let her leave school early and join the family business.

Don was disappointed and was by now regretting his decision to send Sharon to the Italia Conti, believing that the theatrical types she had mixed with had been a bad influence on her. If she had been to a 'normal' school, he reasoned, she might have grown up a bit more normal herself. But whether it was school, her upbringing or simply her genes, normality simply wasn't in Sharon's repertoire. As much as Don wished otherwise, it was far too late to do anything about it. Sharon hated school and felt she was wasting her time.

It was 1967, with all the hope and opportunity that era had to offer, and it was time to move on. Show business was all she had known since the day she was born. Life on the stage might not be for her, but somehow, somewhere, in the crazy world of entertainment Sharon was determined to carve her niche.

CHAPTER TWO

Daddy's Girl

*❝I was taken into the business at fifteen.
That's how things were done.
If my dad had been a butcher
I'd be cutting up lamb chops today.❞*

A S THE RADIO AT HER BEDSIDE blared out the latest pop hits, the teenage girl applied the finishing touches to her lipstick, draped her fur coat around her shoulders and ran downstairs to climb into the Rolls-Royce waiting at the front door. It might have been her first day in her new job as a lowly office receptionist, but that didn't stop Sharon Arden travelling in style.

When her father Don had realized that Sharon was serious about quitting school he agreed that she should learn about life as he had done – in the world of hard graft. He would pay her £12 a week to answer the phones in his office in Curzon Street, in London's Mayfair. It was not the most glamorous job in the world, but Sharon loved it and jumped into the passenger seat of her father's car every morning full of excitement about what the day ahead would bring. And Sharon soon discovered that working for Don involved a whole host of duties not written down in the job description. 'It was more like keeping the phone connected, the electricity on and the landlords from kicking us out,' she later explained. 'If the job hadn't worked out for me, I could've always signed up as a juggler, because that's what I did.' When Don didn't have the cash needed to pay the wages or the bills, Sharon would become involved in elaborate schemes to persuade the bank manager to hand over the money. For a teenage girl, living by the seat of her pants in this way could have been a scary introduction to office life, but Sharon relished every moment, bounding into Don's private office several times a day, full of ideas and enthusiasm.

Yet after just twelve months Sharon's independent streak reared its head. Convinced she could do better and make a living off her own bat, she promptly quit and took the first job she could find, working in a bar. It was not as easy as she had anticipated and it was only a matter of weeks before she was fired for not knowing enough about the different drinks. Undeterred, she applied for a job as a waitress at the Hard Rock Café in the centre of London. This time she didn't even get through the training when it emerged her arms weren't strong enough to carry trays heaped with plates and glasses.

Sharon's confidence took a dive and she dejectedly went back to work for her father. Not close enough to Hope to turn to her for support, and temporarily at odds with her father, Sharon began to comfort eat. She had always loved food, hence her teenage struggles with her weight, but now it became her solace too. 'Cake, fried food, cheeses, anything and everything. Any time I felt a pang of fear, I ate,' she explained.

When she was seventeen Sharon began dating her first boyfriend. He was a good-looking guitar player in one of the bands that her father managed and she fell head over heels. Besotted and with dreams of an idyllic future together, she ended up sleeping with him – the first time she had ever made love with a man. But rather than it being the romantic encounter she had hoped for, she sadly found the whole experience a bitter disappointment. To add to her misery, two months later Sharon discovered she was pregnant. She and Hope had never had any traditional mother-daughter chats about sex education and it was certainly not a subject she would ever discuss with her father. With such limited knowledge of contraception it was almost a sad inevitability that she would end up this way. For any single teenage girl an unwanted pregnancy is a frightening and bewildering experience, but this was 1969 and attitudes were not as liberal as they are today. Added to her despair was the fact that Sharon felt she had absolutely no one to turn to.

In desperation and with tears streaming down her face she eventually plucked up the courage to tell her mother the terrible news, but Hope's reaction was as hard and unfeeling as Sharon feared it would be. Without pausing for breath she coldly announced that Sharon would have to 'get rid of it'. She gave her the name of a local abortion clinic and sent her off there alone the following day. 'I was terrified,' Sharon recalled. 'It was full of other young girls, and we were all terrified and looking at each other and nobody was saying a bloody word. I howled my way through it, and it was horrible. It was the worst thing I ever did.' That evening Sharon went home and went straight to bed, where she spent the whole weekend in her room in constant tears. With little reassurance from her parents she felt utterly alone. As she recalled later: 'My mother's way of dealing with it was she wouldn't talk to me or do anything to help me. That was her punishment.' Sharon went back to work on the Monday morning in abject misery on the inside, but on the outside pretending she had enjoyed a perfectly normal weekend. It was what her parents expected, for as far as Hope was concerned, it was business as usual.

With her sedentary job and her weakness for food, Sharon began to gain weight. In the late 1960s everyone wanted to look like Twiggy. Unable to compete with her slim friends Sharon went the other way, making herself the fat girl who was best friends with all the boys, telling herself that was all she wanted and needed. Yet as loud and jolly as she was on the outside, inside she still craved love. Gradually, as her heartache over the abortion eased slightly, she dated a succession of young men on the fringes of the music industry. Sadly few of the relationships brought her happiness. They tended to be short-lived, often doomed by her father's view that the men just weren't good enough for her.

While her home life and love life were far from ideal, Sharon still took great pleasure in her work. She thrived on being part of the rock industry; music was her passion and she could not get enough of it. Like most other teenagers at that time, her weekends were often spent hanging out at London's fashionable Marquee Club on Tottenham Court Road. It was where the biggest bands of the late 1960s strutted their stuff, where the up-and-coming bands made their names and where would-be performers begged for a slot on the bill. In 1969 a new band by the name of Black Sabbath took to the stage. No one had heard of them, and at the end of the night everyone agreed that they had never seen anything like them, either. Their songs of witchcraft, death and destruction set them apart from their contemporaries and Sharon was immediately captivated. She had not particularly noticed their skinny, long-haired lead singer, but there was something about the band and the singer's distinctive wailing voice that made her sit up and take note. As she recalled, the band had given her goose pimples. 'I was like "What the fuck is this?" It was like nothing else.'

The following year, in 1970, Black Sabbath's second album *Paranoid* gave them a British number-four hit. Sharon, sharing her father's sharp instinct for business, decided it was time Don saw them too. The next time they appeared at the Marquee Club Sharon dragged her dad along. After witnessing their deafening set Don agreed they definitely had something about them. A meeting was quickly arranged in Don's London offices. On the appointed day, the sight of these four outlandish musicians in the flesh was too much even for Sharon and for once her usual bravado escaped her. Four years her senior, frontman Ozzy was wearing a pair of pyjamas and had a tap around his neck attached to a piece of string. They all had thick and very long hair. 'I had to ask them if they wanted tea,' recalls Sharon. 'They all grunted at me and they wouldn't sit on the seats; they sat on the floor because they were hippies. I was shitting myself and I couldn't look at them; I was looking at the switchboard. I was used to all these smooth American stars who were perfectly groomed with their mohair suits and cologne. Then in came these raggedy guys from Birmingham with hair everywhere and I thought, "What the hell is this?"' Don had hoped that he would persuade the band to join him, but it wasn't to be. The band was parting company with their original manager, Jim Simpson, but instead of joining Don's outfit they opted for a new management team of Patrick Meehan and Wilf Pine. Don was upset, but let it go, while Sharon merely breathed a huge sigh of relief that she would not have to encounter them ever again.

By now Sharon was becoming her father's right-hand woman. She was only eighteen but she had grown up fast. She was smart, sharp and had an instinct for the business. Don would frequently rely on her opinions and ideas, increasingly taking her along to business functions with him. But as Sharon soon realized, being the boss's daughter wasn't always quite the perk it might have seemed. 'I'd meet people at receptions and they'd say "Who are you?" I'd say, "Sharon Arden" and they'd go, "Oh, OK, right" and they'd go the other way. It was because his reputation was so fierce, everybody was terrified of him.' Their reaction was understandable, for Don's management style was still as uncompromising as ever. And Sharon, as she grew older, was learning more and more about the way he operated.

By the early 1970s Don was doing so well in business that he was able to move house again. The family moved out of their grand house in Mayfair to an even bigger mansion in leafy Wimbledon, south London. At the same time he moved offices – to a new place he had bought in Berkeley Square. His son David was working for him too now, but it was Sharon – the apple of her daddy's eye – who wanted for nothing. 'He was a very powerful man in the music industry,' Sharon explained. 'And my father had the old way of working, that if you take anything that's mine you're in big-time trouble. But if you're nice with me, I'll be nice with you. I mean, he treated me like a princess. I was a twenty-year-old covered in diamonds and driving a Rolls-Royce. Whatever I wanted he would give me.'

With London and unlimited finances at her disposal, Sharon was by now forging her own reputation – as a party animal. She drove a big car, dressed in diamonds and designer clothes and began hanging out with a hard-drinking, hard-partying music industry crowd, who lived for pleasure. Drugs and copious amounts of alcohol were all part of the scene and Sharon lapped it all up, revelling in every hedonistic moment. Sharon's drugs of choice were tablets called Quaaludes. Hugely popular in the 1960s and 1970s, particularly in the music business, they lowered inhibitions and decreased anxiety leaving users feeling euphoric, relaxed and happy. As she admitted in a candid interview with *Q* magazine many years later, 'Oh God, I was the Quaalude queen. And the drinking . . .'

Frequently Sharon would not make it home at night, crashing out on friends' sofas and in their spare rooms. Such was her capacity for drink that on one occasion she apparently even forgot she was in charge of her young cousin Cathy. According to Cathy, who was only fourteen at the time, she had been invited to London to stay with Don and the family. As Don and Hope temporarily had to go away on business, Sharon had looked after Cathy during the day at work. But at six o'clock she took Cathy back to one of the secretaries' flats and asked her if she would mind looking after her cousin for a couple of hours, while Sharon nipped out. When it reached eleven o'clock it became clear that Sharon was not planning to return that night and the secretary made up a spare bed for the bemused teenager. When Sharon showed up the next morning there were plenty of apologies, but little explanation as to why she had failed to return.

Despite her glamorous party life in London, Sharon would still pay visits to her grandmother in Manchester every few months, calling in to see her Aunty Eileen across the road. But Sharon soon discovered that her free-living London ways were not quite as acceptable in Manchester. Her grandmother Sally was of the old school – with straight-laced Victorian values. By now Sharon had a new boyfriend, a young man by the name of Adrian, who worked for Don. Sharon thought nothing of taking Adrian with her on one of her visits north. Her grandmother was not impressed and when she caught the couple kissing and cuddling on the settee she told Sharon in no uncertain terms that her behaviour was unacceptable. Sharon and the boy were both told to pack their bags and get out, and no amount of pleading by Sharon would persuade Sally to change her mind. Stubbornness was clearly an Arden family trait . . .

Although Don had lost out to his rivals in securing Black Sabbath, Sharon and Ozzy's paths continued to cross. Much to Don's annoyance his son David had become friends with rival manager Patrick Meehan. Patrick threw lots of parties and at his New Year's Eve celebrations to mark the start of 1971, Sharon and Ozzy found themselves chatting. Ozzy was dressed in his own inimitable style, with several crucifixes around his neck, open-toed sandals and jeans, while Sharon as usual was dressed up to the nines with diamonds and a fur coat. By her own admission she was, by now, on the large side. 'Fat, too much jewellery. Too much hair. Too much everything.' Yet despite their very different looks there was an instant chemistry and the couple soon found themselves flirting and giggling. Sharon in particular was bowled over by Ozzy's sense of humour, while the first thing that attracted Ozzy to Sharon was her laugh. He explained: 'She has a really hearty laugh and she's always crazy. I'm always crazy too.'

Emboldened after several drinks Ozzy eventually confessed to Sharon that although he found her attractive, there was a problem about them getting together, because he felt she was way out of his league. Despite his success, Ozzy still felt very self-conscious about his humble roots, while away from the stage he was actually quite a shy person. Sharon meanwhile was outgoing, outspoken and loud and had the image to go with it – fur coats and big cars. Sharon, as down to earth as ever, confirmed that Ozzy was indeed right: there was something stopping them becoming an item. But it wasn't their different backgrounds, it was the small matter of Ozzy's fiancée, Thelma Mayfair. A local girl from his hometown of Birmingham, she had met Ozzy in a nightclub where she worked as a cloakroom attendant. The couple had enjoyed a whirlwind romance and were due to marry that year. Thelma was a divorcée, with a five-year-old son, Elliot, from a previous marriage, but big-hearted Ozzy was already planning to adopt the boy and raise him as his own. Ozzy shrugged and admitted Sharon was right and at the end of the evening the couple parted with a hug, but no plans to meet again.

In 1974 Don and Hope celebrated their silver wedding anniversary with a stylish ball in London's Kensington, with guests tended by liveried footmen. All of Don's friends were there, including show-business executives and musicians from the top bands of the time. Also present were his family from Manchester, including Sharon's cousin Cathy, by now a very pretty teenager who bore more than a passing resemblance to her older cousin. Sharon's boyfriend Adrian took quite a shine to Cathy and asked her to dance. While Sharon was initially pleased that he was being so polite to her family she was not keen for it to continue too long, and when the music stopped Sharon quickly cut in. 'Be careful, she's only fifteen,' she said, smiling sweetly as she firmly whisked Adrian away.

By 1974 Don had set up his own record company – Jet Records. His first signing was the popular singer-songwriter Lynsey De Paul. Lynsey had made her name in 1972 with the jaunty Top Five hit 'Sugar Me', but then things had gone a little quiet for her. Don's first UK single release with Jet was a new song for Lynsey, called 'No Honestly'. The theme to a popular TV comedy series, it shot to number seven in November, revitalizing her career and firmly placing Jet Records on the map.

Don found Lynsey hard to deal with, so he came up with the perfect plan. He already trusted Sharon enough to put his companies in her name. Now it was time to trust her with management duties as well. Lynsey was about to embark on a world tour and Sharon, he decided, would be her tour manager. He assumed, wrongly as it turned out, that Lynsey would appreciate having another woman on the road with her. He also assumed that Sharon would be so pleased at landing such a big job that she would behave impeccably and do anything she could to avoid upsetting Lynsey. Not for the first time Don had underestimated his daughter's larger-than-life personality. The two women headed off on tour together, but it soon became clear they had nothing in common. Sharon was a raucous party animal who loved to stay up late, drink and eat junk food. Lynsey was quiet, more serious and ate carefully to avoid putting on weight. She didn't drink and preferred to spend her evenings quietly in her room.

By the time they reached the Seychelles towards the end of the tour, the pressure was building between them. After the show Lynsey went back to the hotel room as usual, while Sharon retired to the bar with the band and crew. It was a recipe for disaster. Sharon recalls: 'This guy had been buying me drinks all night. I staggered back to our room and Lynsey said, "Have you been drinking?" in this prim and proper voice of hers. And I was like "So what if I have?" Her suitcase was open on the floor, so I pulled up my dress and squatted over it. She was like "Are you pissing in my suitcase, Sharon?" And I'm afraid I was.'

Despite her confrontational style (or perhaps because of it), Sharon was now proving worth her weight in gold to her father. She was young, vibrant and had a good head for business: Don was relying on her more and more. She might only be twenty-three but he could count on her for more sensible advice than from many business associates twice her age. Father and daughter were a double act and whenever Don had an important business trip to make, Sharon now went with him. Yet it was rarely plain sailing. Although Don treated Sharon as a valued member of his staff, she was still his little girl. And woe betide anyone who forgot that. In 1975 on a trip to Midem, the annual music-business festival held in Cannes, Sharon and Don were unwinding one evening in one of the local casinos. After a few minutes Sharon spotted Patrick Meehan Jr at one of the other tables. There was no love lost between Don and Patrick Sr after Meehan had successfully beaten Don to signing Black Sabbath. But just to rub salt in the wound, Patrick Jr had then gone on to have a brief affair with Sharon in the early

1970s. Don hadn't liked it, but what he liked even less were the rumours that had reached him afterwards that Patrick had secretly taped their lovemaking and shown the video to his friends. Don didn't know whether it was true, but the rumours alone were bad enough and he had warned Patrick in no uncertain terms never to speak to his daughter again.

Sharon had become agitated at the mere sight of Patrick at the gambling tables and went on and on to her father about it. In the end, to keep her quiet, Don went over and started to give Patrick a piece of his mind. What he hadn't counted on was Patrick's friends wading in to help him. Within seconds Don found himself on the floor and all hell broke loose, with a number of people – including Sharon – joining in the fight from every direction. The fracas caused such a commotion that the press picked up on it and Don's altercation made the headlines the next day.

In 1976 Don Arden finally took over the band he had coveted for six years: Black Sabbath. The group was hugely successful both in Britain and in America and Don knew that their tours, as well as their records, could potentially make him and the band a fortune. Since their split with their original manager they had continued to be managed by Patrick Meehan Sr and Wilf Pine, but as the years passed the band had become less and less enchanted with them. Patrick had originally toured with the group, but with their increasing success he was spending more and more time at his office. Ozzy felt that Patrick was living it up at home while they were doing all the hard work out on tour and relations grew increasingly strained. Don was by now an even bigger name in pop than when he had first approached the band and this time Ozzy was convinced he was just the man to guide their careers to the next level. They signed on the dotted line and then promptly relocated to America to escape Britain's tax laws.

By now Sharon had become close to Black Sabbath's guitarist, Tony Iommi. They had mutual friends, but although Sharon had a crush on Tony it never developed beyond a platonic, if close, friendship. It was through Tony that Sharon became reacquainted with Ozzy. Black Sabbath was playing a concert at Long Beach, not far from the offices Don had now established in Beverly Hills. Sharon was temporarily over in America on business and Tony persuaded Sharon to go along and see the show. Tony invited her backstage to the dressing room and it was there she bumped into Ozzy once more. Some years had passed since they last spoke, but once more Sharon found herself instantly captivated by him. She found him a fascinating and complex character – crazy and uncontrollable, he had by now developed a reputation as one of the biggest drinkers in the business, with an almost insatiable appetite for drugs. Yet at the same time he was gentle, kind and racked by self-doubt. As she explained many years later: 'He was the wildest of the wild men. And yet he was funny, sweet and attentive. He made a good impression.'

In 1977 Sharon moved to California permanently. Feeling that much of his work and his future now lay in the States, Don had decided to make the country his permanent home. David and Sharon were not only his family but an important part of the business too, and there was never any suggestion that they would stay behind in England. By now Sharon was so successful that Don had trusted her with one of his most important – and lucrative – bands. The Electric Light Orchestra, better known as ELO, had enjoyed a Top Ten hit in Britain in 1973 with 'Roll Over Beethoven' and under Don's guidance had risen to become one of the biggest bands of the mid 1970s. With hits such as 'Livin' Thing' and 'Telephone Line' they had millions of fans on both sides of the Atlantic and a reputation as some of the best live performers in the world. With touring such a big part of the business Don assumed Sharon would be thrilled at the honour of becoming their tour manager. And she was. For a short while, anyway. The problem was that Sharon had developed an insatiable taste for the high life. She had known glitz, glamour and decadence since she was a little girl and had assumed that life on the road with one of the world's biggest bands would be one non-stop round of parties and fun.

But Sharon had not taken into account the personalities of the band members of ELO. She was twenty-five and many of them were a good ten years older. They were not young men thrilled by the prospect of nights in hotels and the opportunity to run wild. They had been performing together for five years and were in it for the long haul. Late nights in the bar, food fights and parties were not their style, and not for the first time Sharon found herself kicking her heels. Just as had happened three years earlier with Lynsey De Paul, Sharon found herself in hotel bar after hotel bar, on her own, while the band retired to bed. As she complained later: 'It was like running an old-age pensioners' club. They'd all been around for years and all they wanted to do on tour was sit in their rooms doing their knitting. I was so bored I would drink just to amuse myself.'

The problem was that her unorthodox childhood had left Sharon with a low boredom threshold and little sense of responsibility. She had seen her father's cavalier attitude to life, money and extravagance and merely copied him. She had a company credit card and she was not afraid to use it. Don Arden recounts how one day, out of the blue, he received a phone call from American Express to check whether he knew that almost £150,000 had been spent on the card in the past twenty-four hours. Don didn't. But he knew a girl who did. Straight away he called Sharon in a rage demanding to know what had happened. The bills included one for £80,000 from Van Cleef, one for £35,000 from Tiffany's and another for £25,000 from Cartier.

Don was raging, but Sharon's reply left him speechless. 'Oh Daddy, I was so bored, I had to do something,' she explained.

Money seemed to mean little to Sharon. At that time she had become close friends with the actress Britt Ekland. Britt and her children and their nanny were regular visitors to the Arden house, and on one occasion Don arrived home to find Britt's nanny wearing the £80,000 necklace from Van Cleef – the one that his money had bought. Not surprisingly he was livid, but when he challenged the nanny she explained that Sharon had given it to Britt as a gift, and Britt in turn had passed it on to her.

When Sharon wasn't giving it away, she was losing it. On tour with ELO she had an argument with the driver of a limo taking her from the airport to her hotel. When she climbed out of the car she refused to tip him and gave him a piece of her mind along with a one-fingered gesture for good measure. 'Bye, you shit,' were her parting words. It was only after the driver screeched off that Sharon realized she had left a case containing her most expensive jewellery on the back seat. She spent two hours trying to trace the driver before she had to leave for the evening ELO show, after which the missing jewellery, worth in the region of £400,000, was promptly forgotten. When a concerned Don quizzed her about the loss she told him not to worry and that the jewels were all insured. A week later when he asked how the insurance company had reacted to the claim, Sharon just giggled. Don recalls: 'She said something like "Oh yeah! I must do something about that . . ." It meant that little to her.'

Over the following months Sharon found herself bumping into Ozzy again and again. As she toured America with ELO and Ozzy toured with Black Sabbath they would occasionally end up staying at the same hotels or meeting at the same parties or music-business functions. He was by now married, but Sharon still found herself drawn to him. An eccentric herself, she loved his refusal to conform, but more than anything she found him funny and revelled in his company. On one occasion Sharon even invited Ozzy to join her and a group of friends for a weekend in San Francisco. Ozzy took this as his cue, but when he arrived it soon became clear that Sharon was not proposing a dirty weekend at all. Instead she saw it simply as an opportunity to get to know him better. Ozzy was initially disappointed, but over the course of the weekend he discovered a side to Sharon he had never seen before. Until then he had always known her as the loud party animal, but suddenly Ozzy realized she had a caring, more sensitive side too. Late one evening when he insisted on staggering off into the night in search of drink and drugs, Sharon sent one of her friends with him to ensure that he didn't stray into trouble. 'That was the point that I had the big attraction for her,' Ozzy recalls. 'But then it took a long time for anything to actually happen.'

With no imminent sign of Ozzy becoming part of her life, Sharon continued to live it up. According to Don Arden's memoirs, in 1978 at a Jet Records convention party, after several glasses of champagne, Sharon and Britt Ekland began to French-kiss in front of a paparazzi photographer. It was nothing more than a silly drunken publicity stunt, but the photographs, predictably, were published all over the world with the suggestion that the two women were involved in a full-blown lesbian love affair. Sharon just laughed it off the next day, but it would take her a long time to live it down and Don was furious. Typically though his darling daughter was not on the receiving end of his rage. Sharon could still do little wrong in Don's eyes, and although he knew deep down that she had got herself into this mess, it was the photographer who received the full force of his fury, in a 6 a.m. phone call warning him to hide before Don killed him.

In October of that year Black Sabbath released another single, 'Hard Road'. It was to be their last record featuring Ozzy on lead vocals. The writing had been on the wall for some time and the band could no longer cope with his self-destructive streak. Ozzy was abruptly cut adrift. With his severance pay tucked firmly in his back pocket he took up permanent residence at the Le Parc Hotel in Los Angeles. The band didn't want him, his wife Thelma didn't seem to want him – not surprisingly, she had grown tired of his absences and his hard-drinking, hard-living ways. With a plentiful supply of whisky and cigarettes, the numbers of the local pizza-delivery service and his drugs dealer, he was more than happy to waste away the hours and days in semi-oblivion. When he became lonely he would wander out to the Rainbow Bar and Grill on nearby Sunset Boulevard and drunkenly chat up a girl. But as the days passed into weeks Ozzy grew more and more despondent. 'I thought it was the end of me,' he recalled in an interview years later. 'I just sat around, getting severely loaded and I thought, "Oh well, I'll be out on the street selling hot dogs in two years' time", you know? Ozzy Osbourne? Who's he?'

Instead, in walked the woman who would save both his life and his career. By 1979 Sharon was managing rock musician Gary Moore, and Gary's drummer Mark Nauseef happened to be staying at Le Parc Hotel at the same time as Ozzy. Mark had an appointment to meet Sharon one day, but he couldn't make it. He needed to give her £300, so he asked Ozzy to keep the appointment for him. All Ozzy had to do, he explained, was hand over the envelope containing the money. Ozzy agreed, but as soon as Mark was out of the door, he went straight out and spent the cash on cocaine.

In his drunken, drug-fuelled haze Ozzy thought he would hear no more of it, but he had underestimated Sharon. She might have started out as her father's receptionist, but the timid little girl so frightened by her first glimpse of Ozzy had long gone. She was now, as her brother David liked to observe, 'Don in a skirt'. Flamboyant and outspoken, she had grown up a lot during the months she had spent on the road with various bands. Nobody, let alone a washed-up singer, intimidated her these days.

The following day Ozzy was woken by a terrible hammering on his hotel room door. Assuming it was housekeeping growing irritated at the permanence of the Do Not Disturb sign, he slowly stumbled out of bed, muttering and swearing as he went. When he opened the door he was almost knocked over as it was pushed back against him. Sharon had arrived. She swept through the place, opening windows and curtains, kicking pizza boxes and throwing beer bottles into the bin as Ozzy cowered in the corner in amazement. He had never seen anything like it. Eventually she stopped and turned to Ozzy, fixing him with an unforgiving stare. 'You motherfucker. You spent my fucking money on fucking drugs, you asshole.'

If Ozzy needed any clue as to what the next twenty-five years would be like with Sharon, that was it. It was his chance – if he wanted – to walk away. He could pay back the money, say goodbye to her and continue on the road to self-destruction. But there was something about Sharon that stopped him in his tracks. There was something about her that captivated him. To his amazement he didn't even mind being shouted and screamed at by her. As he recalled many years later: 'Sharon had my attention. When she starts in with a plan, it's pointless to do anything but listen and agree.'

CHAPTER THREE

A Meeting of Minds

*❛ I hadn't been married – I hadn't even had
a steady bloke before Ozzy. ❜*

I F BURSTING INTO HIS HOTEL ROOM in a flurry of four-letter words wasn't enough of a shock for Ozzy, Sharon's next pronouncement totally stopped him in his tracks. Since leaving Black Sabbath Ozzy had convinced himself that his music career was well and truly over, and during the drunken days and weeks spent alone at Le Parc Hotel he had concocted what he thought was a brilliant scheme. Instead of trying to reinvent himself as a performer, he would go back to England, try to patch things up with his wife Thelma, and run a pub. When Sharon eventually composed herself after her dramatic entrance, he sat her down and earnestly explained his plan, asking Sharon for her thoughts. A smile twitched at the side of her lips, but it was no good, she couldn't keep it in. 'Ozzy!' she shrieked, before she doubled over, giggling hysterically. When she eventually stopped laughing she explained to the nonplussed singer that she couldn't think of anything worse than putting a drunk in charge of a pub: it would simply be the end of him. She had a much better plan. She would take on Ozzy as a solo singer. Sharon would now be his manager.

Don was more than happy with the idea. He had bigger fish to fry than a washed-up singer who seemed to have little future ahead of him. His son David couldn't do it; his baby daughter Charlotte had just been born prematurely and he needed to be with his family. So if Sharon wanted the job it was hers. Don couldn't imagine why she was interested, or how she thought she would make a success of it, but he didn't mind if she wanted to try. Ozzy felt similarly. He couldn't really understand it, or see it working out, but with nothing else on the horizon he was willing to give it a go.

What neither Don nor Ozzy had counted on was Sharon's sheer determination to make something of her new charge. For this was an entirely new challenge for her. Until now she had acted as tour manager for her father's bands, but this time round she was a personal manager, which put her in overall charge. There would be no answering to record-company executives – or to Don. It was her own pet project.

Sharon admired Ozzy's big heart and his talent. And she already had a clear idea of where he was going wrong. 'Ozzy had always bugged me because he was lazy, he was insecure and dumb,' she explained. 'He was like a squashed man, but I knew that he had so much more in there and I was just trying to kick his ass into shape. Stuck in a hotel room in Los Angeles with no band and he just wants to sit there taking drugs. He was just not helping himself. I saw it as an opportunity to take his career in hand and make him a financial success.'

Sharon told Ozzy in no uncertain terms that it was time to clean up his act and that was her first priority. She had found him in a bad way and the final months of 1979 were spent cajoling, pleading, nagging and shouting at him, while she slowly weaned him off the drugs, the drink and the groupies and built up his confidence once more. As Ozzy recalled: 'I think she felt sorry for me. She goes, "If you straighten your act up, I want to manage you." Everybody up to that point was going "You dummy, you idiot, you can't do fuck-all." All my life I used to be called a dummy. She was the one who didn't.'

But Sharon's caring side was combined with an iron will to succeed. And as far as she was concerned, her relationship with Ozzy was strictly business. She certainly had a soft spot for him, but she was determined her personal feelings for Ozzy would not get in the way of her work. Besides, Ozzy was in too bad a shape emotionally to begin a new relationship and he was still married to Thelma, with whom he had had two children, Jessica (born in 1972) and Louis (born 1975). During the coming months he and Sharon built a close bond and working relationship, but that was as far as it would go.

By the start of 1980 Sharon felt Ozzy was ready to face the world. It was time to put together a new band. Using her contacts in the music business she put out word that she was looking for a group of musicians to work on a new solo album with Ozzy, and also a possible tour. Auditions were set up in a Los Angeles studio and Sharon ruthlessly vetted each hopeful, checking how they interacted with Ozzy, what they looked like and how they played. If they didn't fit the bill musically or Sharon felt they had an attitude problem they were given short shrift. Aged only twenty-eight, she had a commanding personality to say the least.

After several days her hand-picked team were assembled: guitarist Randy Rhoads, drummer Lee Kerslake and bass player Bob Daisley completed the line-up. Sharon named them Blizzard of Ozz and flew them to England where, on 22 March 1980, they began work on Ozzy's first post-Black Sabbath album. They set up camp at Ridge Farm Studios in Surrey and by the end of the summer the album was complete.

During this time both Sharon and Ozzy formed a close friendship with guitarist Randy Rhoads. Randy had a depth to him rare in rock musicians, and didn't want to spend every hour partying and getting drunk. The trio instantly gelled and many an evening was spent sitting up until the small hours, discussing their shared love of music and putting the world to rights. When Randy eventually staggered off to bed, Ozzy and Sharon would gaze at each other and smile, both finding it increasingly hard to ignore the passion building between the two of them. Recalls Ozzy: 'She was always a very classy woman, smart and outgoing. I came from a totally different background, not as wealthy or educated, and I thought she was an impressive woman. I was attracted to her, but at that time I was married. My marriage wasn't going well, but I wasn't looking for a wife. Then one thing led to another, and I fell in love with her.'

Yet Sharon, as strong-willed as ever, continued to hide her feelings and whenever Ozzy drunkenly propositioned her she would remind him that he already had a wife and family at home. Inside she wanted him more than she'd ever wanted anybody in her life, but she was just too scared to let him know. During the past few months Ozzy had completely opened up to Sharon about his childhood, his hopes and fears and most important of all, his deep feelings for her. But as touched as Sharon was by his honesty, her own fear of rejection and failure remained. She had been hurt too many times in the past to risk it happening again.

With the band now in rehearsals, Sharon decided it was time for them to play their first gig. She jumped on a train heading for Scotland and within a couple of days had found a tiny backstreet venue in Glasgow and persuaded the manager to take a chance on an unknown rock band called Law. It wasn't much of a place, but for the unsuspecting punters who walked in a week later it was to be a night to remember. Sharon had kept quiet about Law's frontman. Shrewdly she had felt it was better for Ozzy to get a couple of concerts under his belt without the hype and hysteria that would inevitably surround his official opening night. Her gamble proved to be the right one. Ozzy left the stage that night with the cheers of the crowd ringing in his ears and his confidence high.

Sharon decided to strike while the iron was hot and in September 1980 rush-released Ozzy's first solo single 'Crazy Train'. It was followed, a month later, by the release of the album *Blizzard of Ozz* and the dates for his first solo tour of Britain. Fans clamoured to snap up the tickets and newspapers devoted spread after spread to his return.

The couple threw themselves into rehearsals, but the more time they spent together the harder Sharon found it to resist Ozzy's advances. One night, after a long day at Shepperton Studios, they stumbled back to the hotel, where they shared a few drinks in the bar. Not for the first time at the end of an evening, Ozzy invited Sharon back to his hotel room, but on this particular occasion she found herself saying yes. It will come as no surprise to discover that the evening did not feature flowers, chocolates or any traditionally romantic gestures. 'I got her drunk and leapt on her,' Ozzy later admitted. 'I was never very subtle with relationships.' Yet for Sharon their love was the real thing. 'When I met Ozzy who was so truthful and just an honest person, I fell for him hook, line and sinker,' she says. 'Yes, he was a rock-and-roller who did crazy things, but crazy was nothing to what was going on in my house.'

Sharon and Ozzy certainly had a lot in common. Their troubled childhoods and passion for the music business were part of it, but there was a shared respect too. They made each other laugh, admired each other's talents and were both capable of incredible tenderness. This open, warm friendship was something Sharon was not at all used to. Her mother had never been particularly demonstrative and her father had always been too wrapped up in his work to lavish a great deal of love and attention on his children. And although Sharon had had relationships previously, they were never serious love affairs. Ozzy, on the other hand – when he was sober – was capable of immense affection. She trusted him and felt she could completely be herself with him. 'How lucky was I to find Ozzy,' she explained. 'He loved me the way I was. I'd never want to make love with the light on. I would roll myself not only in the sheet, but the duvet and the bloody pillows. But Ozzy would laugh. He'd tell me I was daft.'

Throughout her twenties Sharon had continued to struggle with her weight. The comfort eating had turned to binge eating and when she was stressed she would eat and eat until she was sick. Periodically she would try health farms and diets. These would be temporarily successful and she would control her eating for several months, but then something stressful would happen and trigger it all off again. As a result she was a good deal heavier than she would have liked, but Ozzy, it seemed, neither noticed nor cared; he adored her exactly as she was.

As loving as their relationship could be, it was also capable of descending into drunken chaos at a moment's notice. Ozzy relied on alcohol as much as he ever had and Sharon was more than capable of matching him drink for drink when she wanted to. Her drinking was never a problem in the way that it was for Ozzy. She could go for weeks without touching a drop if she felt like it, but when she did drink she approached it in the same way she approached anything in her life – at 100 mph. If there were a competition to see who could be the last person standing at the bar Sharon would win it. She would drink more and faster and become louder and more obnoxious than anyone around her.

What's more, her drinking was capable of landing her in serious trouble. Just before leaving Los Angeles for Britain, Sharon had been arrested for drink-driving and had to be bailed out by her close friend Britt Ekland. When she woke the next day she had no recollection of what had happened, until Britt reminded her of the incident. If it was a warning sign to slow down, Sharon paid no heed and on tour in Britain she and Ozzy found themselves developing a reputation for their drunken outbursts.

Both had strong characters and quick tempers and were not afraid to vent their feelings, wrecking hotel rooms, hurling furniture at each other and trading insults at the tops of their voices. On one occasion Sharon was so furious that she hurled a bottle of perfume straight at Ozzy's head. Too drunk to get out of the way in time, it hit him full on and a doctor had to be called out to treat him for concussion. Recalls Sharon: 'Our fights were legendary. We'd beat the shit out of each other. At a gig Ozzy would run off stage during a guitar solo to fight with me, then run back on to finish the song. I would drink to keep up with Ozzy. My body just [couldn't] handle it. So I was a terrible drunk. We'd both drink until we blacked out and wake up the next morning with black eyes and bruises – he'd hit me, I'd hit him. We were both in the gutter, morally.'

It was not only Ozzy who found himself on the receiving end of Sharon's temper. Ever since the break-up of Black Sabbath Ozzy had been involved in a war of words with the band's former guitarist, Tony Iommi. The pair had experienced a love/hate relationship during their time together and feelings were still strong. Although Sharon and Tony had been close, that was before her relationship with Ozzy. Now her loyalties were completely to him and his foes were automatically hers. Eventually Sharon decided to act. After phoning Tony for a supposedly friendly chat she discovered that he would be taking a date to one of London's smartest restaurants that very evening. Sharon grinned to herself as she plotted her revenge. That evening, as Tony and his new girlfriend sat down to champagne cocktails, a waiter came over to their table bearing a gift he said had just been delivered to the restaurant by courier. Tony looked surprised – he wasn't expecting anything – but assumed someone from the record company had wanted to thank him for his work. As his curious girlfriend peered over his shoulder he smiled and lifted the lid off the box in expectation. When he saw the contents the colour drained from Tony's face. It wasn't a set of cufflinks or a beautiful watch, it was a pile of faeces. Tony didn't take long to work out exactly who was responsible. As an unrepentant Sharon later explained: 'It was in a Tiffany gift box. He was giving Ozzy a hard time, so I gave him a hard time.'

One morning not unlike most others, Sharon woke up in her hotel bedroom feeling dreadful. As was often the case she and Ozzy had ended the night with a drunken argument. This time it was in the hotel restaurant where they had hurled glasses, plates and insults at each other, in front of shocked diners. Sharon lay in bed the next morning with a terrible hangover and a hazy recollection of what had happened. The fight had been no different to those they'd had in different towns and cities along the way, but this time something snapped and Sharon decided it had to end. She had long since stopped taking drugs and at twenty-eight felt it was finally time to clean up her act completely. 'It got to the point where it was so bad that I had to say, I just have to stop,' Sharon later recalled. 'I realized that if we both carried on, we'd wind up a washed-up pair of old drunks living in a hovel somewhere. And then one morning I woke up and said "One of us has to be together enough to deal with the business." So I quit drinking that day.'

With a clear head Sharon now decided it was time to tackle her growing weight problem. Her love affair with Ozzy had restored her self-respect and her success in the tough world of music had restored her self-confidence. Feeling buoyant, she began a new diet from the University of Boston, which involved substituting powdered drinks for meals. After four months of no fried food or cakes Sharon had shed a staggering eighty pounds. Ozzy thought she looked fantastic and couldn't keep his eyes or hands off her, but then that had always been the way. He had always told her that he found her attractive whether she was fat or thin. He was impressed by her determination to stick to the diet, but was genuinely happy to be with her whatever her shape.

Since Sharon had given up drinking their fights had become less frequent and less violent, and there was now no doubting how much they adored each other. Yet Ozzy remained married to Thelma. In his heart he knew it was over, but every now and then, driven by guilt, he would go back to her and try to start afresh. As much as he loved Sharon he felt bad about the way he was treating Thelma and worried hugely about the impact their split would have on their three children, Louis, Jessica and Ozzy's adopted son Elliot. An emotional man at the best of times, he found it hard to cope and poured his heart out to Sharon night after night, unsure which way to turn or what to do for the best. Sharon dealt with it calmly and patiently, listening to his outpourings and lending a sympathetic ear. 'She had to put up with this dribbling, drooling mess of a person, crying and sobbing and falling all over the place,' Ozzy recalled. 'If it was the other way round, I'd have gone "She's a nutter, I'm out of here." I was in a terrible state for a long while, but she stuck it out with me.'

Eventually Thelma could stand no more of Ozzy's indecision and issued divorce papers. Ozzy was sad, but at the same time felt huge relief for it meant that he and Sharon could now discuss their future together in earnest. He had proposed on numerous previous occasions, but Sharon had firmly pointed out that he was already married and that while she was happy to try most things once, bigamy was a step too far. With his divorce imminent she was finally able to accept. Sharon recalls with a smile: 'He went down on his knee and asked for my hand in marriage. He was very romantic and very sweet.'

Despite the success of the tour Ozzy had very little money. He had already spent most of his pay-off from Black Sabbath and wouldn't see the tour receipts for some months to come. He couldn't afford a lot, but he was determined that Sharon would have a ring to demonstrate his love. After a visit to H. Samuel he chose the biggest and best ring he could afford and headed back to their hotel, but things did not go according to plan. Recalls Ozzy: 'I thought I'd better get some flowers. I was pissed so I nicked them from a gravestone. I gave her this bouquet of flowers and she read the message "In loving memory of George" and realized I'd nicked them from a graveyard and chinned me and threw the fucking engagement ring away.' It was the first of many arguments during their engagement. As soon as Ozzy was drunk the couple would fight, fall out, break up, make up and start all over again the following day. Sharon might not be drinking any more, but that didn't stop her being just as volatile as her fiancé. 'We had five different engagement rings,' she recalls. 'Every time Ozzy would ask me to marry him, we'd have an argument and I'd throw the damn ring out the window.'

With the tour complete Ozzy went to live with Sharon in a cottage in the grounds of her parents' new home, Kimberley House, a large mansion in the Surrey countryside close to Dorking. Yet trouble would flare up even when the couple were meant to be relaxing at home. Ozzy loved to cook to help him unwind and his speciality was stews. What Sharon didn't know was that along with the fresh potatoes and broccoli, Ozzy was adding some special ingredients of his own: drugs, lovingly prepared in the kitchen with the help of a pestle and mortar. Each time Sharon sampled one of these culinary delights she would lose control and smash up the house. She recalls: 'I couldn't control my emotions. It wasn't until months later that he told me he was putting drugs in the stew. It took me a while to get over that, you know.'

Many managers at this stage would have cracked open the champagne, kicked back their heels and been content with success on their home turf, but that wouldn't have been Don Arden's way and it wasn't Sharon's. Sharon was a chip off the old block, and her success in Britain had only whetted her appetite for bigger and better things. With the British tour completed, Sharon now had her heart set on cracking America. At the start of 1981 Sharon flew back to the States. She had restored Ozzy's confidence and re-established him in Britain. Now she was intent on getting him a record deal in America. She had emerged from her alcohol-ridden days as a virtually teetotal workaholic, who was fast making her mark as a manager. She had watched her father's mistakes and learnt from them, but she had also learnt that being tough got you what you wanted. As Ozzy explained, 'The business is run solely by men. When they first saw her, they immediately assumed she was an airhead chick. But once they heard my wife yell and throw things out the window, they went: "Good God! She's the real thing!"'

Sharon travelled alone on this occasion, ordering Ozzy straight back into the recording studio in Britain. She knew that with spare time on his hands he would quickly stray back into his old, bad habits and she would do anything to avoid that. She explained years later: 'All my life I've worked in the rock-and-roll industry, I was born into it and obviously I've been around drug-taking all my life, because so many people in the industry take them, but it terrifies me; it's a one-way street. When I first met Ozzy he was taking a lot of drugs. They were all very, very young and it was like "Oh, let's try it, this is fun" – it was like giving kids toys. But I hate it.'

When she arrived in the States Sharon found to her disappointment that the impact Ozzy had made in Britain counted for little. Both promoters and record companies felt that Ozzy was no longer the star he used to be and Sharon found door after door closed in her face. Not only was she a young woman, but she was also Don's daughter and Ozzy's girlfriend. It meant she had a lot to live up to. It was not going to be as easy as she had hoped. Rather than viewing this as a setback, Sharon became even more determined to succeed and when the going got really tough she proved to be every bit as fierce as her father. 'I had to learn to be very hard with people,' she explained. 'Because it was the only way to break down that wall. As soon as I went in the room, they knew: Don't fuck with me, because I won't take it. So then it became "She's the daughter of [. . .] and she's fucking the lead singer too – she's a cow." Which I actually preferred.'

Verbally Sharon had always been able to fell a man twice her size, but according to a newspaper report, when she felt it was needed she was not averse to resorting to physical violence. After finally managing to secure Ozzy a slot at an American rock festival she discovered to her bitter disappointment that he wasn't topping the bill as promised. Allegedly, she tracked down the promoter and demanded to know why. He started to reply, 'Listen, little lady . . .' He didn't get any further. According to the article, Sharon knocked him out with one punch.

By March 1981 Sharon had persuaded Jet Records to release Ozzy's first solo album in the States, but it was to be with the minimum of fuss and publicity. What's more, they would only pay him £44,000. Ozzy was disappointed, Sharon less so. For by now she had thought up a detailed game plan. Firstly she decided Ozzy had to live up to the superstar status he had earned during his time in Black Sabbath. As a result he would play no support slots for other bands. Instead he would concentrate on heading the bill at smaller 3,000-seater stadiums, however little he was paid. Next she set about re-vamping Ozzy's image. His trademark white catsuit, designed by his wife Thelma, was consigned to the bin. His whole look was too 1970s, Sharon told him. Overnight his hair was dyed blond, he began to wear much heavier make-up, and elaborate, brightly coloured outfits became the norm.

Next came part three of the plan: the publicity. Sharon was a shrewd and astute woman. She had seen how pages of newspaper coverage had helped raise Ozzy's profile and boost both ticket and record sales in Britain. Now she needed to crack the American press. Her opportunity came sooner than she had expected. That summer Jet Records and its distributor, CBS Columbia, invited Ozzy along to one of their regular conventions. These were informal gatherings where record company executives could meet and chat to the bands on their label. Sharon knew that CBS were not actually that interested in Ozzy, having just signed up Adam Ant, who had become a huge star in Britain. In order to make Ozzy stand out from all the other singers there that day, she was going to have to come up with something good. After staying up half the night brooding about it, Sharon decided that Ozzy should walk into the room and pull out three doves from his pocket. She told him to fool around with them for a while before releasing them into the air. It would surprise the record company executives and cause a bit of a stir, and naturally there would be a photographer on hand to capture the moment and release the pictures to newspapers and magazines. It would guarantee Ozzy some much-needed American press attention.

Ozzy was nervous about the meeting and before they had even arrived at the CBS offices he had downed the best part of a half bottle of whisky. It made no odds to Sharon. She handed Ozzy the doves and he hid them in his coat pocket as instructed. When he entered the room he sat on the arm of a chair and after a few minutes Sharon gave him the nod. What happened next took *everybody* by surprise. Sharon says: 'He let two of them fly off and all these silly girls were sitting there smiling and sighing quietly and then Ozzy grabs the last dove and yanks its head off [with his teeth]. I couldn't believe my eyes.' With blood dripping from his mouth on to his trousers Ozzy dropped the dove's bloody, still-flapping body on to the meeting table in front of him. As horrified executives heaved, Ozzy and Sharon were escorted from the building and warned never to come back.

Not that Sharon needed to worry. While the CBS executives might have been horrified by the stunt, everyone else was suddenly clamouring for a piece of Ozzy. The photographs and story, as Sharon had predicted, had leaked out and newspapers and magazines all over the country were soon filled with reports of the outrageous singer. TV and radio stations queued up to interview him. The Humane Society of America started a determined campaign to ban him from performing anywhere in the United States, while his teenage fans revelled in their hero's new-found notoriety. Suddenly everyone had an opinion on Ozzy.

The stunt had transformed his image literally overnight. Sharon could not have anticipated just how far Ozzy would take it and undoubtedly what he had done was cruel and shocking, but from a marketing point of view it was a stroke of genius. Ozzy was no longer just another long-haired heavy rock singer, he was now considered a crazy eccentric. He was someone the media wouldn't dare take their eyes off for a second in case they missed his next outrage. Sharon had wanted to raise his profile and she had done it. It was the couple's first taste of real controversy. And they were enjoying every minute of it.

'It was all so perfect really,' Sharon recalled later. 'We had stayed up until four o'clock in the morning the night before the convention, trying to dream up an idea for something Ozzy could do that would make everyone remember him. And finally, when we came up with doves, I still thought he was half-joking about biting its head off. But believe me, it really worked for us.'

In the autumn of 1981 Sharon took Ozzy back to Britain to cash in on his new-found notorious status, but very quickly things started to go wrong. While Sharon was now staying away from the bar, Ozzy was doing enough drinking for both of them and it soon became clear that he was not in a position to cope with the tour either physically or mentally. The problem was that Ozzy was right in the middle of his divorce proceedings and, as much as he loved Sharon, he found it hard to forgive himself for the way he had treated Thelma. He blamed himself entirely for their break-up and would torture himself with thoughts of how different things might have been.

In Bristol he appeared for an encore wearing nothing but his underwear. The following night in Cardiff the audience pelted him with dead crows. He would think nothing of breakfasting on the contents of an entire mini-bar and at night he would start all over again. One British tabloid journalist recalls how he joined Ozzy in the bar of a hotel in Sheffield for a drink after the show. 'He asked what I wanted as a nightcap. I said a Hennessy brandy. Oz replied: "Great idea," and ordered us a bottle each.'

In Leicester Ozzy suffered food poisoning and cancelled the show, but it was not enough to stop him hitting the Holiday Inn hotel bar that night with Sharon. Unfortunately Don Arden, who had invested in the tour, was furious when he heard what had happened and immediately jumped in his car and drove from London to Leicester to have it out with his daughter.

After berating her for twenty minutes Sharon finally blurted out the news she knew would stop him dead in his tracks – she and Ozzy were to wed. It worked perfectly. Don ordered champagne and the three sat back and celebrated, their row immediately forgotten. After a couple of hours Don headed back to London leaving Sharon and Ozzy to celebrate alone. But not even Ozzy could drink continuously all evening and remain sober and when two uniformed police officers walked into the hotel foyer, Ozzy saw red. Although they were there on another matter and were nothing to do with Ozzy and his party, he was so incensed by their presence that he charged towards them screaming 'I'm gonna do the bastards' at the top of his voice. Sharon quickly grabbed one arm and a journalist the other and they managed to drag him away, but according to a newspaper report things did not remain calm for long. At a table in the bar Ozzy spotted a group of Japanese businessmen. They hadn't noticed him and probably had no idea who he was, but that didn't matter to Ozzy, who promptly picked up a basket of bread and started hurling rolls at their heads. Sharon rushed across to apologize and literally dragged Ozzy off to their hotel room, cursing and yelling at him for his stupidity as they went.

By now Sharon had realized that Ozzy was clearly not up to performing on stage every night in his current fragile state. Bravely she took the decision to cut her losses and cancel the rest of the tour. There was disappointment from the towns and cities that hadn't yet been visited, but Sharon felt it was better to let down a few thousand fans rather than let Ozzy perform below par, news of which would reach millions of people through the media.

She ordered him to America to recuperate, while she set about arranging his next live dates – this time a tour of the States. After arriving in New York she promptly arranged a meeting

Above: A young Sharon in a rare picture from her childhood, *c.* 1960, at her parents' holiday flat at Minnis Bay. Left to right: Sharon, her grandmother Sally Levy, father Don and mother Hope. No one could have guessed that the demure-looking girl would grow up to marry one of the wildest men in rock.

Right: Sharon's future husband, singer Ozzy Osbourne.

Sharon marries her beloved Ozzy on 4 July 1982 in Maui, Hawaii. Pictured left to right: Sharon's parents Hope and Don, Sharon, Ozzy, Ozzy's mother Lillian and one of his sisters.

Ozzy tenderly places a ring on Sharon's finger during the wedding. The new Mrs Osbourne boasted that Ozzy stayed sober during the entire ceremony.

The Prince and Princess of Darkness. Even on their wedding day the couple couldn't resist playing up to Ozzy's stage image.

Left: From Day One Sharon took control of Ozzy's life and career. She is seen here applying his make-up backstage before a concert in 1986.

Right: Ever since she was a teenager, Sharon struggled with her weight – but Ozzy always insisted he loved her, whatever her size or shape. She is pictured here in 1990; it would be another nine years before she took her weight in hand.

Above: Sharon and Ozzy with Aimee and baby Kelly in 1984 in Palm Springs, California. Sharon insisted on moving to the States and making a fresh start just after Kelly was born.

Below: Sharon and Ozzy with all three children in the garden of their home in Hampstead, London in 1987. Left to right: Ozzy with Jack, Aimee, Sharon and Kelly.

Above: Sharon's children never knew a life outside show business. Here they are pictured at the *Kerrang!* Music Magazine Awards, London, in 1997.

Below: Sharon and Ozzy with Aimee in October 1997. Aimee never felt comfortable in the limelight and four years later refused to take part in the TV series *The Osbournes*.

Above: Sharon and Ozzy pose with Kelly and Jack for a publicity picture in February 2002. The two children were about to become household names around the globe, thanks to *The Osbournes*.

Left: Sharon and Ozzy, with some of their many dogs, at home in Los Angeles in 2002.

Above: Sharon's first public appearance since being diagnosed with cancer. Accompanied by Kelly, she accepts an Emmy Award for best reality-TV series for *The Osbournes* in September 2002. In her acceptance speech, in front of a cheering audience, she simply declared: 'Ozzy, I love you.'

Below: Despite her illness Sharon refused to cut down on work. In February 2003 she opened a news conference to announce the twenty-eight-city Ozzfest 2003 tour.

Sharon and Ozzy scream with delight as they leave the Bloomberg party following the White House Correspondents' Dinner in May 2002. Although her success meant the couple were now moving in high-society circles, Sharon was still capable of being as wild and as controversial as ever.

with one of the city's biggest promoters, John Scher. Scher realized Ozzy's potential and immediately agreed to arrange a show for him in the city. He and Sharon agreed terms and neither thought anything more of it, until Sharon arrived in his office a couple of weeks later to collect her payment from him. Unfortunately there was a dispute over the amount of work Scher had put into advertising the show. Sharon argued her corner, but when Scher refused to back down she lost it completely. 'So I got up and nutted him with my head and then I kicked him in the balls,' Sharon recalls. 'He just stood there. He was just so taken aback. And then I pulled on his hair. And I never, ever worked with him again and he never worked with me. So the only way, unfortunately, for me is to get nasty and to get violent. At least you feel better,' she concluded.

The odd setback apart, Sharon worked quickly and effectively and in January 1982 Ozzy and his band were back on the road again. She knew that Ozzy had a lot to live up to, not just musically – this was his first American tour since leaving Black Sabbath – but also following the incident with the doves. She realized that many fans would be coming along simply to see what stunt Ozzy pulled next and she didn't intend to disappoint them.

Enterprisingly, either she or the promoters ordered mailshots to be sent to the towns where Ozzy would be appearing, encouraging concert-goers to bring along raw meat to throw at him during the show. 'It read something like "Bring your liver to an Ozzy show – and he'll throw it back at you,"' Ozzy recalls. What's more Sharon had it written into the contract that each venue would provide £25 worth of calves' liver and pigs' intestines. During the show Ozzy would catapult buckets of the rotting offal at the audience and they in return would hurl pigs' entrails, livers and plastic rats and snakes on to the stage. So on 20 January 1982 at a show in Des Moines, Iowa,

Ozzy thought nothing of it when a bat was flung at his feet. Assuming that it was plastic like the others he bit into it, only to realize that it was in fact real and very much alive. As he recalled: 'Sharon told me later that she saw its wings flapping from the side of the stage, but I didn't. I just picked it up and put it in my mouth in the excitement of the show.' Ozzy rushed off the stage and, while every journalist in the place ran for the phones, for once publicity was not Sharon's concern. Genuinely concerned about Ozzy's health she pushed him into a car and drove him straight to the hospital for a series of rabies injections. The next day Britain and America went into melt-down. Fans rushed to snap up the few remaining tickets and while thousands queued up at every venue to demonstrate against him and denounce him as a Satanist, Sharon was busy adding more and more dates to the end of the tour.

Despite his success Ozzy was drinking as heavily as ever. Sharon, sensing that they were on the verge of something huge with his career, was growing increasingly impatient with his indulgences and the couple were once more fighting like cat and dog. It was a dysfunctional relationship and at times it seemed that the only beneficiaries were the countless florists and jewellers who supplemented Ozzy's regular and flamboyant apologies. Sharon threatened to leave him on many occasions, but at the final push she could never go through with it. She loved him and couldn't imagine life without him, however hard life got. They were by now proving a formidable duo, each complementing the other's strengths. Music commentator Rick Sky, who spent time with them on tour, recalls how they would play up to their differences, with Ozzy asking Sharon's opinion and permission over the slightest thing. 'Sharon struck me then as being his nanny, more than anything else,' Rick recalls. 'He would look at her and say in his strong Birmingham accent: "Is it alright if Ozzy goes and has a little glass of water now, Shaz?"

He's a great character and played up to it, but there was certainly a real sense of dependency. If it wasn't for Sharon I think you could safely say he'd be dead.' As Ozzy himself summed it up: 'One day I said to her "What right do you have to tell me what to do? You can't sing a fucking note." She said: "Maybe I can't sing, but you can't read a fucking contract."'

Meanwhile the tour was going from strength to strength. But as far as Sharon was concerned that was no reason to rest on their laurels. Sustained publicity was still as vital as ever and in February she invited the British weekly rock paper *Melody Maker* out to America to catch up with Ozzy. The band had just arrived in San Antonio, Texas and the photographer thought it would be a good idea to take Ozzy out to the Alamo to pose for pictures. By now Sharon had resorted to desperate measures to prevent Ozzy from drinking when she wasn't around. The tour hotels were always warned in advance that on no account should they deliver alcohol on room service to their suite. In a moment of inspiration Sharon came up with the bright idea of removing all of Ozzy's clothes from the wardrobe. Surely even Ozzy wouldn't dare go out to a bar naked, she reasoned. With nothing to wear he would have to stay in his hotel room, watch TV and drink coffee until she returned.

What Sharon hadn't counted on was Ozzy's sheer determination to get a drink. Even if his own clothes weren't around, hers were. So, decked out in a green evening gown, Ozzy headed for the nearest bar. By the time he remembered his meeting with the photographer Ozzy was completely drunk. He hailed a taxi and arrived at the Alamo, still in his green dress with a bottle in his hand. Unfortunately Ozzy had left the bar in such a hurry that he hadn't had time to go to the toilet; he was now desperate. Looking around he found what appeared to him to be a tumbled-down brick wall, turned his back and relieved himself. In fact he had chosen part of the Alamo – a sacred national shrine in America. All hell broke loose. Stewards had witnessed the event, the police were called and Ozzy was jailed, fined and finally banned from playing in San Antonio ever again.

When Ozzy appeared in court, Sharon was nowhere to be seen. It wasn't that she was ashamed or even embarrassed by what he had done. The fact was that Sharon didn't have time for public displays of wifely devotion. Instead, while Ozzy stood in court mumbling his apologies, Sharon locked herself in her hotel room and hit the phones. Now there was even more interest in her act it wouldn't hurt to organize a few album signings at the major record stores in the remaining cities along the tour. Ozzy's antics at the Alamo would go down in history as one of the most shameful days in the monument's history. What true fan, reasoned Sharon, wouldn't want a memento of that?

CHAPTER FOUR

Family First

❝ People would openly say: 'You and Ozzy won't last.'
They expected him to have a big-titted blonde trophy wife
and he'd got me, a short, fat, hairy half-Jew.
I had a lot to fight against. ❞

AS CLOSE AS SHARON HAD BECOME to Ozzy there had for some time been a third person in their relationship. As the band toured the States in early 1982, Ozzy's friendship with their talented guitarist Randy Rhoads had grown tighter and tighter. But so too had Sharon's friendship with him. So close were they now that Sharon and Ozzy had even discussed what would become of Randy when they eventually tied the knot. They did everything together, talked about everything together and were rarely out of each other's sight. At times it seemed as if Randy was the glue that held their relationship together – gentle, shy, thoughtful and intelligent, he was a peacemaker when things were going badly. To outsiders it seemed strange, but to Sharon it seemed perfectly normal – she loved both men, just in different ways.

Only once, it seems, did it ever spill over into something more with Randy. It was in many ways uncharacteristic of Sharon. Although she had enjoyed several love affairs when she was younger, within relationships she was strictly monogamous. She had never been tempted to stray with previous boyfriends and with Ozzy – the first man she had ever loved – she was even less inclined to look elsewhere. As far as she was concerned Ozzy was everything she would ever want in a man. 'He's a legend,' she explained. 'I admire him and I love him.' The situation with Randy was something different, however. If, as Sharon indicated in *Ordinary People*, something physical occurred between her and Randy, it was an intimacy she found hard to explain at the time and even afterwards, but also something that never for one second threatened her relationship with Ozzy. As she explained later: 'Ozzy knows and has never wanted to discuss it . . . but don't read any dissatisfaction into it. Ozzy knows the one-time occurrence was loving, not lustful.'

The trio kept each other company through the long days and nights of their American tour. But on 19 March 1982 everything was to change. Sharon, Ozzy and the band had played a show the previous night in Knoxville, Tennessee and had spent the night on their tour bus en route to Orlando, Florida. When they pulled up for a break at a bus depot at Leesburg, Florida at 8 a.m., the bus driver, Andrew Aycock, noticed the depot had a small landing strip and some light aircraft. Telling the passengers that he used to be a professional pilot he offered to take anyone who was awake up for a spin. Tour manager Jake Duncan said he would like to go, as did keyboard player Don Airey. After their short flight Aycock returned and went up again, this time taking tour seamstress Rachael Youngblood and Randy Rhoads.

What happened next is not entirely clear, but what is known is that, after circling the bus three times, the plane dived, clipping the bus and crashing into a nearby house, where it exploded into flames. All three people on board were killed instantly. Sharon and Ozzy were devastated and locked themselves away in a hotel room until the day of the funeral. But with the funeral behind them, Ozzy showed no signs of recovering. Not since his father died, in 1978, had he felt so grief-stricken. Randy was only twenty-four and his best friend. In tears he told Sharon that he could not carry on with either the tour or the band. Sharon realized she had to act fast. Ozzy might feel he could no longer go on making music, but Sharon knew that at a time like this music was the only thing that would save him. She explained: 'I knew that unless we got up and did something, Ozzy would be over.'

Three weeks later she held auditions for a new guitarist and three weeks after that she had the band back on the road again. They could not replace Randy, but they had to do their best to carry on. It was not an easy time. The crowds were getting out of control. No longer content with throwing offal they had taken to hurling bottles and explosives at the stage. One night Sharon was rushed to hospital after a firework exploded at her feet. What's more Ozzy was drinking heavily and consuming even more drugs than before to mask his grief. Sharon was running out of patience with him and without Randy to calm the situation, the two would argue and fight more than ever. On one occasion Sharon even threw a potted plant at Ozzy's head when she discovered he had been taking cocaine. As she recalls: 'The only way I could hope to control Ozzy was to literally end up having these horrendous fist fights with him all over America. I'd discover where he'd hidden his awful bag of coke or whatever, and so I'd throw it down the toilet or out of the window. Then he'd find out and he'd beat me up and I'd beat him up and it just went on and on like that for months.'

Despite their problems Sharon still had her heart set on marrying Ozzy. Their original plan was to have a huge heavy-metal wedding back in Britain, with all their family and friends present, but Ozzy's decree nisi, which would formally end his first marriage, had still not come through and in the end Sharon and Ozzy decided they could wait no longer. As soon as the divorce came through they would marry, wherever they happened to be. As Sharon recalls: 'At first we were going to get married in LA and then Ozzy had a tour booked in Japan, so we were in Hawaii when the decree nisi came through, so we said, "That's it, we'll get married here." And so we got married on the beach and it was lovely.'

The wedding took place on 4 July 1982 on the tropical island of Maui. Drummer Tommy Aldridge acted as best man. Don and Hope flew out to be there, as did Ozzy's mother Lillian and one of his sisters. Sharon wore a traditional white wedding gown with a long veil and carried flowers and Ozzy did his bit, dressing in a white suit. Their parents entered into the swing of things by decking themselves out in traditional Hawaiian garlands. But even an event as important as this one was not sufficient to keep Ozzy away from the bar. The evening before the wedding, Sharon decided to have an early night to catch up on her beauty sleep. Ozzy promised he would be along soon; he just needed a couple of drinks to help him unwind. Sharon nodded off and in the early hours of the morning she was woken by the phone ringing at the side of the bed. 'It was the night porter telling me that my husband was lying in the hallway and would I go and get him. So I just left him there,' Sharon remembers.

Ozzy sobered up the following morning and staggered back to his hotel room, where he quickly showered and changed. Sharon had wisely chosen a morning wedding and after the couple had lovingly exchanged vows she was able to boast proudly that her husband had remained sober throughout the entire ceremony. It was shortlived, and that night the couple let rip. After sipping cocktails under the palm trees Ozzy jumped up on stage with the resident hotel band and launched into raucous renditions of his favourite Beatles songs, while Sharon and the other delighted wedding guests danced in front of them. Declared Ozzy afterwards: 'It was a great wedding, the best wedding I've ever had in my life and I don't want another one because you can't top the one I had. I'm desperately in love with my wife and I swear to God it's the best thing that's ever happened. I'm a very proud husband.' Yet as proud as he was, Ozzy could not stop himself getting uncontrollably drunk. Rather than spending their first night together as man and wife curled up in bed making love, Ozzy spent it collapsed in the hall outside their room. As Sharon observed wryly: 'I actually carried him over the threshold.'

Few people outside their close friends and family could see it lasting. They knew of Ozzy's gargantuan appetite for drink and drugs and they also knew he was easy prey for the groupies that followed any big tour. Says Sharon: 'People in the industry were taking bets. There was a big pool going – everyone was putting in £100 – six weeks, six months, nothing more than a year.'

With the wedding over there was no time for a honeymoon – they were already committed to further tour dates and the following day they flew to Japan. If Sharon thought marriage would tame her husband, she had got it very wrong indeed. For not only did the drinking and drug-taking continue, but Ozzy also seemed to think that marriage was no impediment to one-night stands. After the concert in Tokyo Sharon was jetlagged from the journey and the excitement of her wedding, so instead of staying on for the post-show party she headed straight back to their hotel to bed. Ozzy said he would have a few drinks with the band, before following her. Five hours later Sharon was roused from a deep sleep by the sound of giggling at the hotel room door. She opened it to find a swaying Ozzy drunkenly struggling to fit his key in the lock; standing with him was a pretty Japanese girl. Recalls Sharon: 'He was out drinking sake all night and he forgot I was there. They were all over each other and I came out of the bedroom and I saw what was going on and picked a mirror up off the wall and whacked it over his head and kicked her out. It's funny now. It wasn't then.'

After Japan, Sharon and Ozzy returned to America to spend some much-needed quality time together. They had barely stopped touring since getting together three years earlier and were looking forward to a break. But Don Arden had other ideas. According to Sharon, she had told him four weeks earlier that she wanted out of all his companies. Although he had happily let Sharon get on with managing Ozzy, the singer was still officially one of Don's artists and as a result he had profited hugely from Sharon and Ozzy's efforts. Now Sharon wanted a clean break, Don was not pleased and had booked Ozzy a string of further dates in America and also signed him up to complete a live album. Sharon was livid. As far as she was concerned she had done a good job managing Ozzy and had put his career back on track. Not only did she resent what she saw as interference from Don, but she also felt that he failed to understand her husband in the way that she did.

Sharon flew back to Britain to try to sort things out, but tragedy was to strike in the cruellest way imaginable. When she arrived at her parents' house one of their guard dogs attacked her. What Sharon hadn't known at the time was that she was actually pregnant with Ozzy's child. 'The dogs ripped me apart and I lost the baby,' Sharon recalled. 'He [my father] didn't set them on me, to be truthful. Because I had been living in America and not in England the dogs didn't know me. Three of them went for me and just tore me apart. I ran next door to my brother who called an ambulance and got me to hospital.' The relationship between Sharon and her parents had really begun to break down the previous year. In 1981 Sharon had discovered that her father had started a relationship with an American academic by the name of Meredith Goodwin. Sharon was livid and thought Don's behaviour was appalling. What upset her even more was that her mother apparently accepted it. Hope seemed to feel that Meredith gave Don the excitement and youthful companionship she could no longer provide and such was her devotion to her husband that she did not resent the situation. Although Sharon had never been close to her mother, this reaction angered her. She didn't know who vexed her most in this bizarre love triangle and struggled to keep a lid on her rage.

Angry at her parents' unconventional relationship and heartbroken over her miscarriage, Sharon felt backed into a corner by Don's demands and was beginning to see him in a new light. Even so, she confessed: 'But at the same time I loved him. He was my dad.'

Seeing no way out she reluctantly agreed to deliver the live album as part of a get-out deal. She would give Don an album and a few live dates in return for Ozzy's contract and the assurance that she alone would now manage and represent him. Don had wanted a double-sided record – half of it Ozzy singing solo material and half Black Sabbath back-catalogue material. Two consecutive shows were booked at the Ritz Club in New York in September 1982, which would both be recorded. But Sharon decided that Ozzy and the band would play nothing but Black Sabbath numbers. She felt bad that she was letting down Ozzy's fans in this way, but was determined that she would not deliver anything of real worth to her father.

Ozzy was shattered and not in a fit state to tour, but Sharon insisted they go ahead and fulfil that part of the deal too. Not only were they contractually obliged to, but Sharon saw it as the only way they would ever be free of Don. Tired, drugged and depressed Ozzy ploughed on, but the tour was clearly getting to him. On one occasion he went missing for forty-eight hours and returned with a shaved head, with no explanation for his actions. Sharon, as pragmatic as ever, merely went out and bought a range of wigs for him to wear on stage.

When the tour ended in the late autumn of 1982 Sharon was immensely relieved. All she needed to do now was sit down with her father and sort out the transfer of Ozzy's contract into her name. She assumed Don would be reasonable; after all, he was a wealthy man with several successful bands to his name. She was just starting out. Ozzy was her only client and he also happened to be her husband. And she was still, despite everything that had gone on between them, Don's daughter. But it was not enough – according to Sharon, Don refused to give up Ozzy without a fight. Finally, to wrench herself away, Sharon reluctantly agreed to buy out Ozzy's contract for £1 million.

As much as she loved him, she could not forgive her father for this and broke off all contact there and then. After thirty years she had had enough of being an Arden. She was Sharon Osbourne now and wanted nothing more to do with either her father or her mother. As she explained many years later: 'It was an insane life and when I married Ozzy I wanted away. People thought that my father was upset because I was marrying Ozzy. But he didn't give a shit. I was taking his cash cow away and he knew once we were married, that was it. And that is what happened; we left.'

Although Sharon now had her freedom, the financial security she had enjoyed all her life was wiped out in one go. Don felt furious and betrayed, and he was not a man to take things lying down. Meanwhile Sharon had left so quickly that she didn't have time to gather any of her possessions from the guest house she used as a base at Don's property in Beverly Hills. As she recalled later: 'I was excommunicated. I mean, I left with two suitcases, no jewellery, no money, no cars, no nothing.'

Free to make her own decisions, Sharon told Ozzy that he could now enjoy a lengthy break from the road and take some time out to record a studio album – his first in two and a half years. Sharon knew Ozzy inside out and realized that his health had genuinely suffered on the previous tour and that what he needed right now was a proper rest. But she was also a shrewd businesswoman, one step ahead of the game. She was aware that after the disappointment of the live album the fans would be desperate for some new Ozzy material. If he was given time to recharge his batteries he would be able to deliver a new album that was fresh and full of the traditional Ozzy spark. It was a clever move.

Many in the music industry had dismissed Ozzy and Sharon as the odd couple: the weird rocker and his seemingly suburban wife. Sharon still battled with her weight and now she hid her dissatisfaction with her size behind large, shapeless dresses. It succeeded in giving her the appearance of a rather timid, mumsy housewife, but nothing could have been further from the truth. Sharon was thirty now and had chalked up an impressive fifteen years in the music business. She had started at the bottom, learning at the feet of her father, and had slowly but surely worked her way up. She had forged a reputation as one of the most driven managers in the business. So driven that many found her just as intimidating to deal with as they had her father. Yet that wasn't how Sharon saw it. 'I'm pretty reasonable,' she explained. 'If I were a man I'd just be seen as this great toughie businessman. I'm a woman, so men say "Oh, she's a bitch."'

With some time on their hands Sharon and Ozzy decided to settle down for a while and create a proper family home. Their dire financial situation meant they could not afford a swish house in the Hollywood Hills, even if they wanted one. But money aside, Ozzy had his heart set on living in England. He missed his adopted son Elliot and his children Jessica and Louis from his marriage to Thelma, and wanted to see more of them.

Cut adrift from her family Sharon felt she no longer had any ties anywhere. Her brother David lived mainly in Los Angeles, but as he worked so closely with Don they no longer spoke. She had kept in touch with her family in Manchester as best she could during her time on the road with Ozzy, but her relationship with them had become a sad casualty of the rift between her and her parents. As far as she was concerned Ozzy was her family now and wherever he felt comfortable she would make her home.

The couple scraped together enough money to put down a deposit on a tiny cottage in Staffordshire, just a short drive from Ozzy's children. Then, with family on their minds, they set about trying to create one of their own. Motherhood, until now, had never been on Sharon's agenda. Her unusual childhood and strained relationship with Hope had not left her with an idyllic view of family life. She had not enjoyed birthdays and Christmas and childish games and cuddles in the way that most children do and had no idea just how rewarding parenthood could be. Work had provided all the fulfilment she could wish for. Her miscarriage earlier in the year, however, had awakened feelings she had never anticipated. It had made her realize that with Ozzy she did want to settle down and enjoy a less turbulent life at home.

Immediately they started to try for a family, but tragically Sharon suffered two more miscarriages. After undergoing various medical tests to find out the cause of the problem it emerged that the abortion she underwent at seventeen had somehow damaged her cervix. Doctors corrected it with a cervical stitch and told Sharon there was now nothing to stop her getting pregnant immediately. They were right: 1982 had barely ended before Sharon started to suffer morning sickness. She rushed out to buy a pregnancy test and to her delight discovered that she was expecting.

The first five months passed problem-free and Sharon felt so well she even went out and got herself a job, working first as a cleaner, then as a barmaid, before finally securing employment as a shop assistant in Marks & Spencer. She had not had a conventional job since her brief and unsuccessful stint as a barmaid when she was a teenager, but with no money coming in Sharon felt she had no choice. 'It was that or starve, basically,' she explained. 'When I left my father, I left everything. Ozzy was broke because he'd just gone through a divorce, so we had nothing. And it was "We make it or we fucking starve." And I end up working at Marks & Spencer. I didn't have a plan. I didn't have anything. I just went feet-first and bulldozed my way into it.'

But in May Sharon's doctor ordered rest for the final four months of her pregnancy and reluctantly she was forced to give up her job. There was no immediate concern, he told her, but after her previous three miscarriages he felt she should not be on her feet working in a shop all day. It was a difficult time for Sharon. Ozzy was now spending a lot of time in the studio working on his third solo album, *Bark at the Moon*, and Sharon found herself stranded in the countryside where she knew no one. But on 2 September 1983, the waiting proved worthwhile with the birth of Aimee Rachel Osbourne.

Sharon was overjoyed and hoped that the latest addition to the family might bring about some sort of reconciliation with her mother. While she could not forgive her father for the way he had behaved over Ozzy's contract she had never actually fallen out with her mother. Their estrangement had been a gradual thing. And while Sharon was still angry that they had never enjoyed a normal mother–daughter relationship, the birth of Aimee had softened her considerably. With Ozzy back in the studio just a few days after Aimee's birth and no friends in the neighbourhood, Sharon did what any daughter would do in those circumstances: she rang home. 'I called her and begged her to come and help because I didn't know what I should do,' Sharon explained afterwards. But if she had expected a tearful and happy reunion, she was to be bitterly disappointed. As far as Hope was concerned Don came first. And if Sharon had fallen out with Don, then she could not expect a warm reception from Hope either. 'She told me to go fuck myself,' Sharon recounted later. 'I really resented my mother. She didn't take care of me in the way that I wanted. In fact, she was an old bat.'

On top of coping with a new baby, Sharon was also overseeing the release of *Bark at the Moon*. For the album's front cover she had come up with the idea of having Ozzy made up as a werewolf, complete with fangs, talons, long hair all over his body and a prosthetic nose. The whole transformation took six hours of painstaking work – each hair on his body and head had to be glued individually and the wig alone cost £2,000. And Sharon, despite having a three-week-old baby, could not resist nipping along to the studio to see how work was progressing. Photographer Ken Lennox, who had been invited along to take pictures throughout the day, recalls: 'Sharon arrived with this tiny baby wrapped in a shawl. Of course it was only three weeks since she'd had the baby so she looked quite mumsy and she was initially very quiet and stayed in the background. When I asked if I could borrow the baby for a photograph with Ozzy she very carefully placed Aimee into Ozzy's arms so he wouldn't scratch her with his long talons. She was very good-humoured about it all and thought it was a great idea for a picture – she instantly understood what we were doing. She stayed on after the pictures were taken and chatted for hours. She was very pleasant and very funny.'

The album was released in December, and within three months

of Aimee's birth Sharon was pregnant again. 'Every time Ozzy and I look at each other, I'm pregnant,' she joked. Their second child, Kelly Lee Osbourne, was born on 28 October 1984. Yet if a second baby daughter was a shock for Ozzy, it was nothing compared to what came next. For when he returned to the hospital to collect his wife and new child the next day, Sharon dropped a bombshell. She had tired of living in the back of beyond in Staffordshire and she had also finally tired of Ozzy's all-consuming appetite for drink and drugs. With a new baby in the family she wanted a new start. She and the two girls were moving back to America, to live in Palm Springs, California, she announced. Ozzy would be flying with them, but rather than heading directly for their new home he would be going straight into the Betty Ford Clinic, high in the mountains at Rancho Mirage above Palm Springs.

Sharon had had enough. When Aimee was just three months old and Sharon newly pregnant with Kelly, Ozzy had left her and headed to the States for his biggest tour to date. Sharon had booked Mötley Crüe as his support act, which had turned out to be a huge mistake. The band had a reputation as a great live act, but an even bigger reputation as party animals and without Sharon by his side Ozzy went completely off the rails. Day after day Sharon would receive phone calls recounting his latest embarrassing escapades: arrested in Florida for peeing in the street, arrested in Tennessee after being found staggering drunk in the street, turning up in restaurants wearing a dress and appearing on stage in stockings, suspenders and a bra – the list went on.

Her husband's antics were bad enough when it was just the two of them. Now with two children to consider things had to change. Ozzy was almost thirty-six and could no longer behave like a naughty child, with Sharon mothering him and picking up the pieces. She needed him to be there by her side, acting as a father and husband. But he couldn't do that with his dependence on alcohol. The world-famous Betty Ford Clinic had helped a host of celebrities rid themselves of their drink and drugs habits and Sharon was convinced it was just the place to sort him out. Ozzy typically didn't really have much of a say. It was a drastic step because Sharon could dearly have done with Ozzy by her side at such a time, but she knew in her heart that she was doing the right thing. Ozzy finally had to face up to his demons. For his own sake, for her sake and for the children's. As she explained later: 'Kelly was four months old and being wheeled around the Betty Ford Centre. The kids have always known what [drugs do] and they know they're not going to get away if they mess with [them].'

CHAPTER FIVE

Married Strife

❝ People shudder when they think of what Ozzy's wife and children must be like. They expect some blonde bimbo with plastic boobs, in black leather and studs and little children with pointed ears and fangs. But when they see me and the kids, they're always surprised. ❞

SHARON WOKE ON NEW YEAR'S DAY 1985 and allowed herself a contented smile. Her babies lay sound asleep in the room next door, her husband was at her side and back from the Betty Ford Clinic. With no alcohol or drugs in his system, Ozzy was all the things he used to be – kind, loving, thoughtful and generous. Motherhood suited her more than she could ever have imagined and she was successfully managing to combine it with her managerial work. She still felt terrible sadness that at such an important time of the year she was unable to pick up the phone and speak to her parents, but otherwise she was blissfully happy. She had a proper family of her own now – something she had never imagined possible.

Sharon had tentatively booked Ozzy to fly to Rio de Janeiro later that month to appear at the first ever Rock in Rio festival.

It was Ozzy's first public appearance since his stay at the Betty Ford Clinic and Sharon was characteristically blunt about the threat a concert like this would pose to his new-found sobriety. 'Rio is the cocaine capital of the world,' she admitted in an interview just before they flew out. 'But I'm going with him and I'll follow him around like a shadow, carrying a big stick.'

Her determination worked and for a while things were relatively calm. Photographer Ken Lennox, who was invited out to take pictures of Ozzy for the *Daily Express*, was struck by how normal day-to-day family life actually was. Ken was due to stay at a local hotel, but when Ozzy picked him up at the airport it was with strict instructions from Sharon to take him straight back to their house. Ken recalls: 'I thought [with her] having a new baby the last thing she would want was guests, but she insisted. When I got there she joked and said: "I wanted someone fucking sane in the house with me!" Despite the sleepless nights she was very personable and good fun to be around and you could see straight away that she brought the humanity to the house. Ozzy was off being the wild man and she was very much the wife and mother; she held it all together. She was sensible and calm and definitely the boss. In many ways it was very much like staying with an ordinary family. Ozzy wore everyday clothes in those days and when he wasn't off being wild he could be very matter-of-fact, and Sharon at that point was obviously very baby-orientated – she looked like a picture-book version of a nice, cuddly mum. They only swore occasionally and they were quite a normal couple. The house wasn't grand and the only sign of staff was one housekeeper and a friend who was helping out.'

The couple had only been in California a short while before Sharon decided on a move back to Britain. They quickly found a beautiful old house in the smart north London suburb of Hampstead. It needed a lot of renovation work, but given time

Sharon sensed it could be the perfect family home. In the meantime they rented a large house off Berkeley Square, one of the capital's most exclusive addresses. While Sharon spent her days looking after the children and supervising the work on their house, Ozzy went back into the studio to start work on his new album, *The Ultimate Sin*. But being back into his old routines he very quickly returned to his old drinking ways. He had accepted he was an alcoholic after his stay at Betty Ford and so now, whenever he slipped off the wagon, he was well aware of the seriousness of what he was doing. It meant that Sharon not only had a drunken and hung-over husband to contend with, but also one full of self-loathing. The situation reduced her to tears on many occasions – tears of both rage and despair. She had just discovered she was pregnant and felt disappointed that things appeared to be spiralling out of control again. As Ozzy candidly explained: 'She tried very bravely to accept me and my addiction, but with two kids it wasn't the life she'd pictured.'

Despite the stress she was under, Sharon ploughed on with her work. In the early summer of 1985 she received a phone call from former Black Sabbath member Terry 'Geezer' Butler, telling her that Irish singer Bob Geldof was putting together a charity concert to raise money to ease the famine in Ethiopia. It was to be called Live Aid and it would be the single biggest pop event in history. Black Sabbath had been asked to re-form with the original line-up and appear on the bill. Sharon knew little about Geldof, other than that he had previously been the lead singer of successful punk band The Boomtown Rats, but instinct told her this would be a huge success. She told Terry she thought it was an excellent idea and set about the arrangements. Black Sabbath were booked to play the American end of the show and Sharon and Ozzy decided to travel to the States in style, booking themselves and their children places on the *QEII* ocean cruiser. Ozzy arrived for the show feeling relaxed and ready to perform his heart out. When they took to the stage he did not disappoint. Sharon had ensured his image was exactly right for such an occasion and on 13 July Ozzy appeared from the wings in a huge purple and gold cloak, sending the audience of millions worldwide into a frenzy of excitement.

Sadly for Sharon the joy of being part of the pop event of the century was marred by the ongoing feud with her father. She had heard nothing directly from Don since their falling-out, but with the music industry being such a small world, she frequently heard word back that he was still unhappy with her and was not prepared to welcome her back into the family in any way, shape or form. As if to prove it, Don had arranged for a writ to be served to the couple backstage at Live Aid – the second Ozzy finished his final song. It attempted to prevent Black Sabbath appearing on stage with Ozzy and alleged that Sharon and Ozzy were attempting to re-form the original group as a performing unit and were actively discouraging the band from having anything to do with Don, their former manager. Don technically still managed Black Sabbath and was annoyed that the Live Aid performance had been arranged by Sharon, without contacting him. Ozzy thought the whole thing was crazy; he had no intention of a Sabbath revival when his solo career was going so well, but Sharon understood the thinking behind the writ exactly. It was a warning aimed at disrupting Sharon and Ozzy's lives and a reminder that Don was still around. He clearly had not forgiven her for taking Ozzy away from him. This was his way of telling her he had not forgotten either.

Sharon put her unhappiness to one side and threw herself into family life once more. She and Ozzy had always dreamed of a large family and their third child, Jack, was born on 8 November 1985. Sharon took three months off work to be with the new baby, while Ozzy completed his album. Sharon adored being a mum and enjoyed every second of her time at home, bonding with her baby boy. But as she eased herself back into work, preparing for the February launch of *The Ultimate Sin*, she was brought back down to earth with a bump.

Both her father and brother had recently been arrested following the kidnapping of former Jet group accountant Harshad Patel. In separate trials at the Old Bailey in London in 1986, Don was charged with false imprisonment and blackmail, while David faced a charge of conspiracy to kidnap and blackmail. The court heard accusations that Patel had been taken to Don's London home, held overnight and beaten and threatened in an argument over money. While Don was found not guilty, David ended up serving seven months in jail. Sharon was utterly horrified. Although she now had nothing to do with David or her father, the case and the ensuing publicity dredged up many unhappy memories and made her realize just how estranged the family actually were.

To add to her woes, she and Ozzy had legal problems of their own. Two years previously an American teenage boy, John McCollum, had shot himself in the head. The last record he had listened to before he died was Ozzy's 'Suicide Solution'. Grief-stricken, his parents had now launched a lawsuit against Ozzy and his record company. Sharon and Ozzy were devastated by the news. They found it shocking and upsetting that a young fan had chosen to kill himself after listening to one of Ozzy's songs, but at the same time they could not accept that anyone would hold them personally responsible. Ozzy found himself besieged by reporters and TV crews, but for once Sharon wished they could both just hide away. As she explained: 'I don't believe that all publicity is good publicity. We don't need this. The industry doesn't need this. Once you start with Ozzy, you start with everyone in TV, in film – where do you draw the line?'

What made matters worse was that the case would not be resolved speedily. Sharon hired the best lawyers she could afford and with heavy hearts she and Ozzy tried to concentrate their minds on work. Ozzy's lengthy 'Ultimate Sin' tour was about to start across the States and Sharon was going too, with Aimee, three, Kelly, two, and Jack, less than a year old, all in tow. When Sharon announced her intentions to the road crew there were a few raised eyebrows, but for Ozzy and Sharon it seemed the perfect solution. It was the way Sharon herself had been raised as a child – she had travelled all over the world – so to her it seemed normal. As Ozzy explained to journalists: 'Circus folk bring their children up that way, so why not us?'

It was to be the family's pattern of life for many months to come. As one tour ended another would begin almost immediately – America, Canada, Britain, Japan – Ozzy was in demand all over the world. Each time Sharon would simply bundle up her family and put them on a plane to the next destination. It meant exciting times for the three children – on the road there were no rules and no strict bedtime – but Sharon was determined that as unconventional as their lives were, they would not be witness to any of the excesses of the rock-star life. On the tour bus Sharon would convert two of the bunks into cots for Kelly and Jack, while Aimee would snuggle down with her parents and watch videos until she fell asleep as the bus trundled through the night to the next venue. During the day the children would be confined to Ozzy's dressing room to keep out of harm's way. Sharon would briefly allow them loose during the sound checks, when they would run around and hide behind the drum kits, playing chase along the rows of seats in the empty auditorium. When Ozzy took to the stage at night Sharon would let the children watch from the wings with her, and when he went back out on stage for his encore, he would frequently take the children with him to mop up the applause and wave to the crowd. It must have been a bewildering sight for children so young, but if they were thrown by the experience they never showed it. They revelled in the fun and excitement of it all. If anybody found the situation stressful and difficult, it was Sharon, who was left with the unenviable task of trying to juggle work and family in the confined area of a tour bus. 'It was a nightmare,' she later admitted. 'What they needed was a secure environment, but what they got was constant change. We had a run of ear infections, colds and sore throats, but I had to do my best while managing Ozzy at the same time.'

Between tours Sharon tried to compensate for the chaotic time on the road, creating the kind of fairy-tale home life that she had missed out on as a child. It meant an almost immediate move back to the country. Sharon had enjoyed her time in London and had even taken keen dancer Aimee along to lessons at the Italia Conti Associate School in Guildford, Surrey. But she now felt it would be better for Aimee, Kelly and Jack to be raised away from the hustle and bustle of the city. She felt that she had grown up too quickly herself and wanted a different sort of upbringing for her own children – something calmer and more idyllic. She and Ozzy found the perfect house near Chalfont St Peter in Buckinghamshire. A twenty-roomed Edwardian mansion, it had a large garden where the kids could run around and make as much noise as they wanted.

Back at home Sharon was in her element. Away from touring and the temptations of drink and drugs Ozzy was the perfect dad: up at 7 a.m. to serve up Rice Krispies and bacon sandwiches before driving the children to school, and in the evenings he would potter around the kitchen cooking roasts, stews and curries for their tea. He even took time to build them a huge tree house. 'When we're home, they're all Ozzy thinks about,' Sharon said proudly. Her view was perhaps a little rose-tinted. Ozzy did indeed adore his children and relished every second with them, but at heart he was a rock-and-roller. And after a couple of weeks of domestic life he would be climbing the walls with frustration, begging Sharon to arrange another tour for him. Sharon would oblige and the family would pack up their bags and hit the road once more.

For a while the lifestyle suited them all, but as the children grew older Sharon felt more and more that it was simply not practical to take Aimee, Kelly and Jack along too. While she had not enjoyed her own schooldays, she felt it important that her children have a stable education and that was something that would never happen on the road. From now on Ozzy would travel alone and she and the children would stay at home. The new set-up worked, but not for long. If Ozzy grew restless deprived of his music, Sharon also grew frustrated if she was kept away from her work for too long. As much as she loved being with the children, she found her job exciting and fulfilling; it was a part of her identity and always had been. Nothing could change that. What's more, as Ozzy's manager she really needed to be with him for long periods of time on the road. Faced with the difficulties of juggling her situation, and with no family support, Sharon decided it would be best to leave the children with a succession of nannies. The children would then fly out to join her and Ozzy during school holidays.

When the children found out about the new arrangements they pleaded with her to change her mind. Kelly would write heartbreaking letters which always began: 'Dear Mummy, please do not go to America and see Daddy.' As distraught as Sharon was about the situation, she could see no way around it. Naturally she did her best to ensure the people she employed had her children's best interests at heart – interviewing them, checking their references and using her mother's instinct about their motives – but things did not always go according to plan. On one occasion she caught a nanny holding Kelly in a head-lock and forcing vegetables into her mouth. On another she found Kelly licking the kitchen floor after being ordered to by one particularly sadistic nanny, whom Sharon grabbed by the head and threw out of the house. But the troubles did not end there. One morning the Osbournes' housekeeper turned up to find the three children locked in a large cupboard – another nanny had put them in there for the night while she held a party in the house. Sharon, who called in the police on that occasion, said afterwards: 'You make the best decision you can. Then something happens and you realize you've had a psychopath on the loose in your house. People are such bullshitters.'

Yet more often than not the nannies would quit of their own accord. They would do their best to tame their unruly charges, but few would last more than a couple of months. Their lack of staying power was understandable – domesticity Osbourne-style took some getting used to. The chaos of life on the road meant that the children did not always settle down well to home life on their return; accordingly mayhem was often the order of the day. They were undoubtedly their mother's children. Spirited and unconventional, they would shout, scream, play practical jokes and run around at will, refusing to respond to requests that they eat regular meals at regular times and go to bed at a reasonable hour.

As difficult as this made life for Sharon, constantly having to rush back to Britain whenever the family ran into more child-care problems, she had no regrets about her decision to stay on tour with Ozzy. It wasn't just that she felt her husband needed her by his side to manage him: to deal with the promoters and agents and make sure he arrived at the right auditorium at the right time. It was also growing increasingly important to keep him on the straight and narrow.

Ozzy had always found it difficult to stay away from the temptations of drugs, drink and groupies. But in his late thirties, rather than slowing down, his capacity for self-destruction seemed to just grow and grow. And as much as he loved Sharon, when he was full of booze and pills he would think nothing of falling into bed with the nearest girl around. Sharon was not happy with the situation and would hit the roof when she found out, but when she had calmed down she was sanguine about her husband's infidelity. She had known since she was fifteen years old that most rock stars behaved this way, given half a chance. She had witnessed it the world over countless times and was realistic enough to understand the temptations. She didn't like it, but at the same time she did not see it as a threat to her marriage. 'What are you going to do when you're away from home and there are girls knocking at your door?' she said once. 'If there had been one person he'd constantly called or had a secret relationship with . . . but he didn't remember their names, faces.'

By now Sharon and Ozzy had received the welcome news that the lawsuit against Ozzy regarding the young fan's suicide had been thrown out, but the relief only sent Ozzy back to the bottle. He would drink when he was happy and drink when he was sad. Sharon tried everything she could to stop him – pleading, cajoling, reasoning and, inevitably, yelling and cursing. Nothing worked. Back at home, he would frequently disappear on 'lost weekends', popping out for a drink on Thursday night and not returning home until the following Wednesday, in a dreadful state. When he did come back they would fight bitterly, chasing each other from room to room, trading punches and throwing whatever came to hand. The next day, full of remorse, Ozzy would head for Tiffany's in London to buy Sharon a diamond ring or necklace by way of an apology.

It was a crazy way to live and Sharon knew that; she just couldn't figure a way out of it. Instead she tried her best to ignore the chaos at home and buried herself in work to escape. She had looked after Ozzy's career for so long she could do it now with one hand tied behind her back, so, in need of more challenges and as a way of saving her sanity, she decided to add a number of other clients to her management stable.

She began in 1987 by signing up sexy American female singer and rock guitarist Lita Ford. Lita had already released three solo albums in the States, with limited success. When she and her record company decided to part, Lita chose to switch managers too, hooking up with Sharon. Under Sharon's wing Lita's career finally took off. In 1988 she released the album *Lita* and hit the American charts for the first time with the single 'Kiss Me Deadly'. It was a massive hit for her and paved the way for a US tour. The follow-up, 'Close My Eyes Forever' – a duet with Ozzy – took her even further, reaching *Billboard*'s Top Ten.

The song had come about in the most unexpected way. On a visit to Los Angeles Sharon and Ozzy had called by at the recording studios unannounced to deliver a house-warming present for Lita, who was in the process of moving apartments. Their choice of gift was typically off-the-wall – a life-sized inflatable gorilla from the San Diego Zoo. They opened a couple of bottles of wine and sat around chatting and playing pool, but after a while Sharon grew bored and went home. Meanwhile Ozzy and Lita started messing around with the studio instruments and gradually began putting together a song. Completely drunk, they persevered until they had finished, by which time it was daylight. The next day Sharon was far from happy that Ozzy had stayed out all night with Lita, but when she heard the song she had to concede it was a fantastic ballad and would work well on Lita's album. She was less happy about the idea of releasing it as a single. As far as she was concerned Lita and Ozzy were two completely separate artists and she wished to keep it that way, marketing them as separate identities. In the end record-company pressure and the reaction of the fans forced Sharon to back down. She capitalized on the success, signing

Lita up for countless press interviews as well as major tours with Bon Jovi and Poison, but she was adamant that the connection with Ozzy would end there and that they would not be appearing live together. Lita was disappointed, but was magnanimous about the situation. 'Sharon worked really hard for me, made me a platinum artist and she's one of the best people I've ever known, but at the end it was a weird situation. We had the big hit, but it just wasn't promoted for some reason,' she explained.

On a roll, in 1989 Sharon signed up British heavy-metal band The Quireboys. She had spotted them at the Reading Festival two summers previously. Under her management the group quickly rose to the top of the UK rock scene and earned a major record deal.

Sharon enjoyed her success and saw it as an added bonus that it upset the chauvinists in the music industry who continued to malign her. They had never taken Sharon very seriously anyway, and when she had become a mother they had assumed she would finally pack up work and become the little wife at home.

But it wasn't just Sharon's success that was making record executives sit up and take note, it was her reputation too. Word had spread that Sharon was not someone you crossed lightly. There were tales that she had sent faeces in Tiffany's boxes to several more of her foes since Tony Iommi and, while no one knew whether this was true or not, few wanted to put it to the test by pushing her too far. When she and The Quireboys eventually parted company, the band's guitarist Nigel Mogg was able to confirm that Sharon was every bit as scary as the stories said. According to an interview with him on a website (www.strangers-in-the-night.com/nigelmogg.htm), 'Don't mess with Sharon,' he warned. 'The last thing she said to me was "I'm gonna cut your balls off and shove them down your throat you little ****!"'

Yet the irony was that Sharon looked anything but tough on the outside. Most days she dressed like an ordinary middle-aged, middle-class housewife on her way to shop at Marks & Spencer – in large billowing skirts and conventional blouses. Since having the children she had gained more and more weight. 'And then I got to the stage where I was like, "Oh who cares? I'm married, I've got kids." So there goes another ten doughnuts in,' she admitted. According to music commentator Rick Sky, Sharon never felt under any pressure to alter her appearance. 'She was in the background and Ozzy was soaking up the limelight. She wasn't a rock-star wife and she didn't need to look glamorous. She had a secure relationship with Ozzy and she wasn't threatened by the groupies; I think she knew that Ozzy would never leave her, he owed her too much.'

As successful as Sharon was becoming in business, she was finding it increasingly difficult to cope with Ozzy. As Ozzy himself admitted: 'My first marriage had been blown out by alcohol and drugs and I was doing a good job on the second one too. Sharon dealt with it by not saying anything. It was worse than a bollocking. She'd just say "Come on kids, we're out of here."' Sharon would disappear for days on end, taking the children with her to stay with friends or even in hotels. Time and time again she would vow she was leaving Ozzy for good because she couldn't take any more, and when things were really bad she would threaten to divorce him, but after a few weeks apart she would miss him so badly that she would come back. 'And I'd think – well, you're unhappy when he's not with you, so you might as well take the miseries and the happiness.'

But inside, Sharon's self-esteem was slowly being destroyed by Ozzy's abusive behaviour. Gradually she had begun to lose the will to fight back. Always by nature a confident and strong woman who stood no nonsense from anyone, she had let Ozzy get under her skin; he was her Achilles' heel. Because she cared so much about him she would let him get away with behaviour she wouldn't tolerate for one second from anyone else. When he was drunk or stoned he would swear at her, threaten her, even hit her; he'd crash around the place, knocking things over, and eventually pass out unconscious.

In the music world Sharon had a reputation as a sharp-tongued, no-nonsense ball-breaker. But at home it was a different matter. She knew that the first time she had forgiven Ozzy for behaving outrageously when he was drunk she had sanctioned him getting away with it again and again. Now she was at a loss about what to do. She could leave, but she loved him too much and could not bear to break up the family in that way. Her main aim became shielding her children from the worst excesses, but it was not an easy task and more and more she began to wonder whether their marriage had run its course.

She and Ozzy had always been chalk and cheese. While Ozzy preferred to spend his nights in bars, or slumped in front of the television watching MTV, Sharon liked classical music, the opera, shopping and sentimental movies. He drank beer, she drank Perrier. He loved tattoos, she hated them. Yet Sharon had never felt such differences mattered. They shared the same goals, the same sense of humour and were in love. Those were the things that mattered, but now Sharon was beginning to doubt that even love would see them through.

With no family to talk to about her problems, Sharon began to turn in on herself. She managed to present a happy face to her children, but when they were out of the house, and particularly in the evenings, she turned to the comfort of food. Feeling she had lost control over her life she would sit alone at night tucking into cheese sandwiches, crisps and cakes. With no one around she would eat and eat until she was sick, repeating the process sometimes up to three times a day. The bulimia took its toll and when she stood on the scales Sharon was shocked to discover that she had reached twelve and a half stone – her heaviest ever.

Yet if Sharon thought things were desperate then, she had no idea what was around the corner. In the summer of 1989 came one of the blackest days of her life. In her early years she had endured the agony of an abortion and miscarriages and the painful disintegration of her relationship with her mother and father. But nothing would come close to hearing the man she loved telling her that she was about to die. In an interview with American *People* magazine in July that year, Sharon had told their reporter that living with Ozzy was like living with several different people. 'One day he can be loving and romantic, but the next day he'll turn into this Jekyll and Hyde monster. I never know what I'm going to wake up with.' She hadn't meant it entirely seriously, but her words would prove to be a terrible prophecy. In August Ozzy travelled to Russia to play at the Moscow Peace Festival. It was an ironic choice considering the state of their marriage, and even more so considering the festival had been staged to raise money for people with drink and drugs problems. But Sharon in all honesty was just glad to have Ozzy away from under her feet for a few days. She decided to stay at home to arrange her daughter Aimee's sixth birthday party; Ozzy would travel alone. In hindsight, it was perhaps not the wisest of decisions, for when the organizers offered a gift of Russian vodka as a thank you for each performer, Ozzy ended up travelling home with a whole case.

The following Saturday Sharon made Ozzy promise to be on his best behaviour for Aimee's party. To everyone's surprise he succeeded – until lunchtime anyway, at which point he decided to toast his daughter with a glass of his new Russian vodka. Of course, Ozzy couldn't stop after just one glass. After drinking the contents of four full-sized vodka bottles he peered blearily into the bottom of the box, hoping he might have missed something. He couldn't believe his luck when he spotted, amongst the packaging, a wide selection of different-flavoured vodka miniatures. Within less than an hour he had drunk the lot and was rampaging around the house, shouting, swearing and crashing into furniture. Sharon quickly sent the children to their beds. She had lost count of the number of times she had seen her husband drunk in the past, but sensed that something was seriously wrong this time. 'It sent him crazy,' she recalls. 'He really did go mad. It was terrifying. I mean, me and my old man have had fist fights before, we've broken up rooms and all that, you know. But never anything like this.'

After his drunken rampage Ozzy calmed down and disappeared into the kitchen for a while, where he began mixing a concoction of drugs with a pestle and mortar. When, a short while later, he finally went upstairs Sharon breathed a sigh of relief. She cleared up the debris and settled down on the sofa with a book for a quiet evening. She hadn't heard a peep from Ozzy and assumed he had passed out drunk on the bed, as he so often did. Suddenly Sharon heard footsteps on the stairs. She turned round to see Ozzy, a glazed expression on his face, wearing just his underpants. Wild-eyed and incoherent he stumbled towards her and grabbed her by the throat, saying: 'I have voices in my head. We've come to a decision. We've decided that you've got to go.' As Sharon recalls: 'And then he just dived on me and got me down on the floor and was just strangling me. But he was gone. There were blinkers on his eyes. He had gone. It wasn't Ozzy.'

Ironically, the elaborate alarm system Sharon had insisted on, because she was frightened of being in the house without Ozzy while he was on tour, was about to save her life. There were panic buttons in every room. Sharon reached across and instinctively hit one of them, alerting the police. Within minutes police cars roared up to the house and a kicking and screaming Ozzy was handcuffed and bundled off, while Sharon sat crying on the floor.

The next day Ozzy awoke in a police cell in Amersham jail to the news that he had been arrested for attacking his wife. He was horrified. He genuinely had no recollection of what he had done and a young police officer had to break the news to him. 'He was terrified,' Sharon recalls. 'Can you imagine waking up and being told that you had tried to kill your wife the night before?' Ozzy spent the weekend in the cells and on Monday morning he was taken to court to be formally charged with the attempted murder of his wife. When Sharon walked into court she felt numb. It was almost impossible to believe this was actually happening. That morning she had made excuses about Ozzy's absence to her children and then sent them off to school as if it were a perfectly normal day. Sharon bitterly wished it were. Her marriage had always been eventful but she could not understand how it had come to this: her own husband accused of trying to kill her.

Yet despite it all she could not face the thought of seeing Ozzy jailed. Although she had feared for her life she reasoned that he had not been himself. She had spent the weekend alone agonizing over what to do and she had finally come to a decision: she would not be pressing charges. Instead she suggested to the court that Ozzy should receive treatment for his addictions. To her delight the judge agreed and that day Ozzy was sent to Huntercombe Manor, an expensive rehabilitation centre in Buckinghamshire. He would stay there for three months before being brought back before the courts for further assessment. The court order further prohibited him from going anywhere near his family during that time, or even phoning them.

Ozzy was crushed; he was convinced his actions would now finally give Sharon the strength to leave him. He was desperately sorry and somehow needed to make a grand gesture to prove his remorse to her. He wasn't allowed out to go shopping, and ordering flowers would have been woefully inadequate. So Ozzy decided to send Sharon one of the things he held most dear in all his life – his hair. Borrowing a pair of scissors he chopped it all off, put it in a box with a note simply saying 'Sorry' and sent it to her. When Sharon opened the box she shook her head, shed a few tears and concluded that Ozzy really was in the best place possible right now.

CHAPTER SIX

Retirement Sucks

❝ My whole life I'd done whatever my father wanted me to do and took care of him. I took care of my husband and protected him and I was kind of exhausted and I said, 'No more'. ❞

WHEN SHARON APPEARED ON ITV1's *Parkinson* chat show in October 2004, the veteran interviewer asked her about Ozzy's attempt to kill her. Sharon, who already had the studio audience eating out of the palm of her hand, was not going to lose them. 'We forget about that now,' she said, waving her hand dismissively. 'Michael, it was just a little strangling, I mean nothing much!' she joked.

Predictably everyone laughed. But back in 1989 Ozzy's attempt on Sharon's life was no laughing matter. It had left Sharon very much on her own. While Ozzy was struggling with his demons inside Huntercombe Manor, her parents still had nothing to do with her and Sharon had three young children, aged six, five and four, to bring up single-handedly. It was difficult to know what to do for the best. Her friends had naturally assumed the marriage was over and told Sharon in no uncertain terms that she would be crazy to stay with a man who had tried to kill her. And after a while Sharon began to feel they were right. But how had it come to this? How had *she* ended up a battered woman in fear of her life? It was time, Sharon decided, to take control once more and stop being a victim.

There was little she could do about Ozzy or her parents, so she decided to make a start on herself. She needed to do something to recapture her lost confidence and put her back in the driving-seat. She began by working out at the gym and dieting. As the weight fell off Sharon's strength slowly recovered and she began to feel more positive about the future. She even went so far as to consult a lawyer and draw up divorce papers. 'And then when it came down to serving Ozzy the papers, I just couldn't do it,' she recalls. 'I was stubborn. And I kept thinking, "I can change him, I can change him. I can change him. I can make it better."'

Clutching those thoughts Sharon eventually decided to visit Ozzy, taking the children with her. It was painful for the couple and simply confusing for the children. As Ozzy later recalled: 'They kept asking me "Why are you here, Daddy?" I didn't know what to tell them. It nearly broke my fucking heart waving goodbye to them as they all drove off.' Yet Sharon kept up the visits, feeling that the heart-to-hearts with a sober Ozzy were having a postive effect. When his three months were up, Ozzy returned to the court to be told, to his relief, that he was a free man. More importantly, Sharon was willing to take him back home and give him another chance. 'He was totally insane from all the drink and drugs he was doing, and well, these things happen,' she said by way of public explanation.

Privately, Sharon was not so forgiving and when they got home she explained to Ozzy that he was now living on a final warning. 'Rehab kind of changed everything because when Ozzy was away getting his life together I got my life together in a different way. I turned the tables and I said I was never going to be in this position again,' Sharon recalls. She made it clear that if Ozzy ever laid a finger on her again she would immediately call the police and it would be the end of their marriage for good. She would not be a victim any more. Knowing the consequences Ozzy did all he could to change his ways. He told Sharon he would try not to touch drugs or drink again, but Sharon was realistic. She knew Ozzy had battled with the bottle for twenty years and was not expecting miracles overnight. Ozzy was making an effort and that was all she asked. As she explained later: 'If you love somebody, you just can't help but love them and they can do whatever and I would just keep on forgiving. I didn't want it to be over and it wasn't a matter of pride, because I don't think you can have pride when you've got three kids together. You see people who have been married three, four, five times and you think – how did you ever find that many people that you really like? I never liked that many men enough to want to marry them.'

After the momentous events of 1989, Sharon decided that 1990 would be a quiet year on every front. She didn't want to overstretch Ozzy who, despite his stay at Huntercombe Manor, continued to fall off the wagon in spectacular style every few months. Apart from a low-key tour with Black Sabbath bassist 'Geezer' Butler and a six-song album *Just Say Ozzy*, she persuaded him to spend a lot of time at home, playing pool or just relaxing with her and the children.

It was perhaps just as well, for even while at home Ozzy was still making controversial headlines around the world. In New York, on 9 March 1990, Cardinal John O'Connor made a controversial address at St Patrick's Cathedral where he lambasted heavy-metal rock music as 'pornography in sound'. Although he didn't name Ozzy he linked rock groups to cemetery desecrations, perverse sex, and demonic possession. Sharon and Ozzy knew nothing about it until Sharon read the shocking headlines associating Ozzy with devil worship. She quickly ushered the children out of the room and sat down to read them in detail with a bewildered Ozzy. When she had finished she could see the look of hurt in his eyes. Despite his stage image she knew her husband was a gentle man, with no interest in the occult or black magic. She felt angry and upset that his name was being blackened in this way. Not only that, but she knew there would also be a knock-on effect on the children. Although she tried to shield them, she could not wrap them up in cotton wool and she knew that this latest story would simply give the other children at school yet more ammunition with which to hurt them. As Sharon said angrily: 'I want to get my hands on this man. He thinks he's doing good, but he's damaging a lot of people; my people that I care about.'

Sharon had been fiercely protective of her brood since they were born. Like any parent she hated to see them hurt or suffering, but there was more to it than that. As a child she had never felt that her own mother cared much one way or the other what happened to her. She had always had to fend for herself. When she had given birth to Aimee, Kelly and Jack she had vowed to be the mother she'd never had – someone who would stick up for her children and defend them no matter what, even if it meant fighting their battles for them. And she had stuck to her resolution. According to Kelly, on one occasion she had returned home from a classmate's birthday party with a black eye. A boy had asked if she was Ozzy Osbourne's daughter and when she'd told him she was he'd punched her in the face. When Sharon found out she was understandably livid. Typically, a phone call to the boy's parents would not suffice. As Kelly recalls: 'So Mum went to this kid's house and beat the shit out of the father.'

Although Ozzy couldn't claim to be completely free of his addictions, he was making an effort to keep his drinking and drug-taking under control and Sharon felt reassured that their wild roller coaster days were behind them. So confident was she that Ozzy could cope that early in 1991 she decided to take the children away for a short holiday to visit one of her friends. Her friends had been a great support when Ozzy had been away in rehab and Sharon felt sure that Ozzy would manage for a week on his own. Perhaps predictably it did not work out that way. When she returned home the following Sunday she found Ozzy lying in his bed, sweating, thrashing around and shouting incoherently. He seemed to have no idea where he was or what was happening. When he eventually calmed down he was able to tell Sharon that the second she had walked out of the door he had started drinking and taking every drug he could lay his hands on. By the Friday morning he felt so ill and disgusted with himself that he had decided to go cold turkey – hence the state Sharon had found him in two days later.

What was needed, Sharon decided, was a fresh start. It was time to move and Los Angeles seemed the perfect choice. Sharon had no contact with any of her relatives in England and as much as she loved London, she was growing tired of commuting back and forth between Britain and America. Most of her business contacts were in the States and although Ozzy was still a huge star in Britain, he was in even greater demand there.

Only one thing worried her about upping sticks and emigrating – her children had settled well in their local schools and had responded to the discipline imposed. Bad language, for example, was forbidden, which impressed Sharon. She and Ozzy might let fly at home occasionally, but she did not want her children cursing as though it was an acceptable everyday occurrence.

As Aimee later recalled: 'They were very strict with that when we were younger. And English schools, you say, like, "hell" and you're out of there.'

Despite what they had been through Sharon was, if anything, closer to Ozzy than ever before. He was immensely thankful to her for the support she had showed him during the past few difficult years and showed his gratitude in the only way he knew how: through his music. His latest album, *No More Tears*, released in September 1991, contained a poignant love song for Sharon, 'Mama, I'm Coming Home'. Mama was his pet name for Sharon (she in return called him Daddy) and the phrase was one he would say to her on the phone towards the end of every tour.

Sharon found a nice house in Beverly Hills and, once the family had moved in, she was intent on getting the Ozzy show back on the road. Now things had apparently settled down at home it was business as usual. Sharon booked Ozzy some concert dates, but in November 1991, to their disappointment, he had to cancel the remaining performances after breaking four bones in his foot while performing one of his famous frog jumps during a song. The following summer the rearranged dates were announced. But to the horror of his fans the tour was no longer called the 'No More Tears' tour. Sharon had renamed it the 'No More Tours' tour. These would be Ozzy's last live performances ever, she told the press. He was retiring from the music business to spend more time at home with his family.

The rock world was shocked. Sharon was a tough operator and they found it hard to believe she would let her star performer quit so early in his career. Ozzy was only forty-three, after all. Sharon must be holding something back; there must be more to the story than she was letting on. There was. And it wasn't just the press that Sharon was keeping in the dark; it was Ozzy, too.

At the start of 1992 Sharon had noticed that Ozzy had developed a strange limping walk. Naturally concerned she had taken him straight to a doctor, who had referred them to a bone specialist. Unable to find the cause of the problem he had sent them to a neurologist who ordered blood tests, a full brain and body scan and even a spinal tap. When the test results returned the neurologist called Sharon into his office and delivered his grim verdict. He was terribly sorry to have to break the news to her, but he feared Ozzy might have multiple sclerosis.

Sharon was devastated. After all she and Ozzy had been through as a couple, she could not believe that fate had dealt such a terrible blow once more. It was a particularly cruel irony that the diagnosis came after Ozzy had been free of drugs and drink for more than a year. It was the longest he had stayed sober since she met him – now it seemed to count for nothing. Sharon had no idea who to turn to, but the one thing she knew for sure was that she could not tell her husband. She knew the shock would be too much for him and would very likely send him running for the bottle once more. Instead she told Ozzy that the doctors thought the problems were caused by years of abusing his body. For that reason, she told him, he should make this his last tour.

Ozzy was surprised, but he went along with it. He trusted Sharon's judgement completely and, as he would tell anyone who would listen, as far as his career was concerned, she was the boss. Ozzy set about the tour with his usual enthusiasm, suspecting nothing. But gradually he began to notice a change in Sharon. Ordinarily tough and cool, he would often find her in tears for no apparent reason. And, normally the biggest fan of his exuberant performances, she had asked him not to jump around so much on stage.

It was months later before Ozzy discovered the agonizing secret burden that Sharon had been carrying around with her.

During a meeting with Epic Records in New York, Sharon was asked if Ozzy had received a second opinion about the problems with his leg. He hadn't, so the record company promptly organized a consultation with one of the country's leading experts. Ozzy was playing in Detroit the next night and Sharon booked a Lear jet to fly them straight from Detroit to the specialist in Boston. Ozzy, by now impatient and angry with Sharon's strange behaviour, refused to go, but when she broke down in tears and pleaded with him, he reluctantly caved in. Once there, the specialist asked Ozzy to walk up and down the room, examined him and then ran a series of tests. Within a couple of hours he delivered his verdict: Ozzy definitely did not have the muscle-wasting condition MS. Sharon was overjoyed; Ozzy was simply bemused. He couldn't understand what all the fuss was about. It was only later that night, when the two of them were alone, that Sharon broke down and explained exactly what she had been through, and the prognosis she had taken on her shoulders in order to protect him. Once again Ozzy contemplated just how incredibly lucky he was to have such an extraordinary wife.

Having already announced his retirement, Sharon decided that rather than explain the suspected MS diagnosis, it would be better for Ozzy to stick to his original story and take some time off anyway. He finished his tour on 15 November 1992 and then headed for home. Many wives would have assumed that having their husband home would mean an extra pair of hands around the house, but Sharon was nothing if not realistic about Ozzy. She knew it would be dangerous for him to have all that spare time on his hands and that he would not stay content for long. Predictably, it happened all too quickly and soon Ozzy was disappearing from home again and hanging out in bars. He agreed to yet another stay in a drying-out clinic, but like previous visits it only worked temporarily.

However, Sharon didn't have time to worry about Ozzy for long – she had other concerns on her mind. After falling out with her father, Sharon had assumed that they'd never speak again and that would be the end of it, but over the years she had heard word that Don continued to tell people in the music business how disappointed with her he was. Sharon would not stoop to her father's level. Besides, she was upset rather than angered by the feud. But that did not stop her exacting her revenge in the most spectacular way possible. Driving through the streets of Los Angeles one day to take her children for Sunday lunch, she suddenly spotted her father and his girlfriend Meredith walking down the street. It was ten years since she had last seen him, but the sight of the man who had caused her so much misery was like a red rag to a bull. Aimee, Kelly and Jack were aged nine, eight and seven, but that didn't stop Sharon. She pulled up alongside the couple and started yelling. Self-restraint was not Sharon's strong point and when Don shouted back at her, she snapped. As she recalled afterwards: 'I was like "I'm going to kill him." I did a big U-turn in the road and the kids were saying, "Mum, what are you doing?" I swung the car round and went up on the pavement and then my eldest daughter said: "Mummy, why are you trying to kill Tony Curtis? Mummy, why is Tony Curtis calling you a whore?"'

Sharon had told her children that both her parents had died in the war and they had never asked any more questions. When they saw Don, with his thick grey hair, they had mistaken him for the ageing film star. Sharon did not have time to explain. 'I said: "It's not bloody Tony Curtis! Shut up, sit down and put your seatbelt on, I'm going to kill him!"' A startled Don and Meredith managed to jump out of the way, but when the car started to reverse towards them at full speed, they realized Sharon meant business and literally ran for their lives.

After the incident Sharon sat her children down and explained the truth about her bitter feud with her parents. She told them that Don was actually alive and well in LA and that Hope was still in England. It was as well she explained, for the road rage attack was not to be her only brush with them, as Don Arden made clear in his book *Mr Big*. A few months later Sharon had arranged to meet a business contact in the Polo Lounge of the Beverly Hills Hotel. To her horror, when she walked through the door she saw her father sitting there enjoying lunch with Meredith. Many people faced with such a potentially explosive situation would have simply turned on their heel and left, but walking away wasn't Sharon's style. Sharon marched up to the table in a fury and started to argue. Don tried to calm her down, but when Meredith unwisely joined in, urging Sharon to sit down and join them, it was the final straw. Sharon turned to Meredith, unleashed a string of expletives, then picked up the shocked woman's bowl of soup and emptied it all over her lap. Don said afterwards: 'It was an embarrassment to me that my own daughter would do something like that to her. But you couldn't convince Sharon that this wasn't the right way to behave in public.'

In 1993 Sharon and Ozzy returned to England again. Now Ozzy wasn't working there was less need to be in America, and Sharon was concerned that in Los Angeles there were far too many people far too eager to provide Ozzy with drugs. More importantly ten-year-old Aimee was not particularly happy at her dance boarding school and wanted to study at dance school in Britain. It was time, Sharon thought, for yet another fresh start. They packed their bags and moved back to their house in the Buckinghamshire countryside. Sharon had always felt it was important to keep a base there and now her inclinations had been proved right. Ozzy told a sceptical Sharon that he would spend his time as a house husband. Aimee was away at her dance boarding school, but Kelly and Jack were at an age when they particularly appreciated having their father around and Ozzy took to his new role immediately, taking the children to school every morning. He spent hours playing with them, camping out with them in the vast grounds at weekends and splashing out on toy jeeps that they could ride around the grounds. But when the children were in their lessons, Ozzy would pace the house, unable to occupy himself. 'I'm one of these people that when I'm on the road I want to be home and then I get back home and do that for a while and end up crawling the walls, itching to get back out there. One thing I discovered is that you have to have something to retire to,' he explained. Ozzy's retirement was getting on both his nerves and Sharon's, but having announced it so loudly and so publicly, Sharon felt they should stick to it. Ozzy couldn't go back on the road but, she reasoned, there was nothing to stop him sitting at home and quietly writing a few songs.

As for Sharon, she was quite content to spend some quiet quality time at home with her family. She had always lived life at full pelt, never stopping to take a breath. Now aged forty, she was enjoying the different pace for a change. Financially they were secure. They were not multi-millionaires, but their success in recent years certainly meant they could enjoy a luxury lifestyle and some time off without worrying about the bills. Always animal lovers, Sharon and Ozzy had acquired five dogs and Sharon would spend her days walking them through the grounds or tending to her children's various needs. Aimee, now eleven, was at boarding school, but Kelly and Jack were ten and nine – an age when they increasingly needed their mum around. Not just for help with homework and to ferry them back and forth to friends', but to talk to every night when they came back from school for their tea. Sharon had never learnt to cook – her mother had never taught her and her lifestyle with Ozzy hadn't involved spending quiet nights at home, where she might have been tempted to try. But she wanted the children to grow up in an old-fashioned English house, where they would return every night to the smell of home cooking and freshly baked bread and cakes. There was only one thing for it, and it didn't involve buying a pinny and cookery book. Instead, Sharon told Ozzy proudly, she had come up with the best solution possible – they would hire a chef.

Despite being back in England, Sharon had no desire to catch up with her mother. Hope was still living at Kimberley House in Surrey and Don would stay there whenever he was in the country, but his work dictated that much of his time was still spent in Los Angeles with Meredith. Although Sharon resented Meredith and was furious with her father, she had little sympathy for her mother. In her own times of crisis her mother had failed to be there for her. At the time it had hurt Sharon badly, but now she had simply hardened herself to avoid any more pain. She still saw nothing of her brother David and his wife and daughter, and had not contacted her relatives in Manchester on her return to England. Ozzy, Aimee, Kelly and Jack were her family now. They came first in her life and she didn't need anyone else.

It was clear Ozzy felt the same. Ever since they had met, people had speculated on the nature of Sharon and Ozzy's relationship. On the surface they were complete opposites. The smart, intelligent and conservatively dressed Sharon, versus the ponderous, long-haired, drug- and drink-obsessed rocker. Yet behind their wildly different appearances they were kindred spirits. Both had experienced unconventional and unsettled childhoods – although Ozzy was raised in poverty in Birmingham and Sharon had enjoyed everything money could buy, they had both hated school and never felt akin to the other children. Unconventional, they clicked the instant they got to know each other. They laughed at the same things and shared the same outlook on life. Yes, they fought terribly at times, but publicly they were one and they would defend each other to the death. As Ozzy explained in an interview with *Rolling Stone* magazine at the time: 'I have a romantic notion that if you truly love somebody, you love them as a spirit as well. My wife and I were meant for each other – she's the only woman I've ever really loved. We have arguments, we throw things at each other, and then we're lovers again. You know, when I see these stupid TV shows, "Mr and Mrs Smith have been together for thirty-nine years and never a foul word between them," I think, "You must be fucking bored out of your mind."'

By 1995, after more than a year at home, Sharon felt there would be no harm in Ozzy putting his new songs to practical use. She called a couple of his old musician friends, Steve Vai and Bob Daisley, and asked if they fancied flying to Paris to work on what would become Ozzy's new album, *Ozzmosis*. Sharon trusted Ozzy to travel alone – although he occasionally lapsed into booze he seemed to have succeeded in giving up drugs completely – and so she decided to stay at home. She was enjoying family life in Buckinghamshire and really didn't want to have to give it all up and leave the children with another nanny simply to act as Ozzy's nursemaid. But by the end of the year Sharon had changed her mind about the quiet life. The lure of life on the road had persuaded her once more. For in truth it wasn't just Ozzy who found touring such a thrill. From organizing each and every gig, to overseeing the promotion and marketing and merchandise, Sharon relished every second. It was the business she had known since she was a teenager and she did it well. She had enjoyed her time at home with her children, but she missed the excitement of work. She longed for the buzz.

But how to explain Ozzy's about-turn over retirement? Sharon thought about it for several weeks before hitting on an ingenious solution. Ozzy had tried retirement, she would tell the press, but had hated every second. With the ingeniously titled 'Retirement Sucks' tour, Ozzy and Sharon were back on the road again.

Very quickly it became clear that things would not be easy this time round. Whether it was his age – Ozzy was now forty-six – or whether it was sheer bad luck, he was plagued with health problems. After a three-car pile-up in Houston, Texas, he suffered whiplash, but that was only the half of it. Sharon, to her frustration, was forced to cancel show after show when Ozzy succumbed first to bronchitis then flu and fatigue. She had put so much into organizing these concerts and, while she sympathized with Ozzy's predicament, she couldn't help but feel his lack of fitness and health problems were to a certain extent self-induced. When he suffered a severe asthma attack in Vancouver it was the final straw. The show had to be cancelled after two songs and a shaken Ozzy was prescribed Ventolin and told to take two sprays a day. Never one for moderation, Ozzy began to increase the doses dramatically. When Sharon found him in the dressing room one night suffering severe palpitations she realized the extent of his abuse. Sharon demanded an explanation and when Ozzy admitted he had taken the drug fifty times that day, Sharon hit the roof. 'I was so wired that Sharon threw all my inhalants out of the window and threatened to kick my ass if I ever took any more again,' Ozzy recalled.

With a lot on her plate, Sharon's patience was wearing thin. She had been growing increasingly exasperated with Ozzy's support band Korn and in the end had decided she could take no more – she threw them off the tour. With Korn sharing the same record label as Ozzy, the following day she was bombarded with phone calls pleading with her to change her mind. When even Ozzy asked Sharon to reconsider she reluctantly agreed. The following day the band's tour manager – the man she held partly responsible for the mess in the first place – approached Sharon backstage with an outstretched hand and a wide smile. He clearly hadn't heard of Sharon's reputation and had no idea what was coming next. As Sharon recalled: 'This idiot comes up and touches me and says: "Oh, I am so glad that Ozzy managed to convince you that you were wrong." And I said: "Get your fucking hands off me – nobody touches me." This guy's about six foot four. And he didn't take his hand off my shoulder. So I kicked him in the knees and he went rolling down the stairs and I said: "You fuck off now and take that fucking band with you."'

In the summer of 1996 Sharon arranged for Ozzy and the band to co-headline the hugely successful Monsters of Rock festival at Castle Donington. It had taken some persuasion but the organizers eventually agreed, only on the understanding that the popular rock band Kiss would share equal billing with Ozzy. Sharon and Ozzy had spent the week before the show in the States on business and flew in to London's Heathrow airport on the morning of the show, from where a taxi drove them up the motorway to Donington. In hindsight it was a mistake for Ozzy to take part. He was jetlagged and hung-over from a sleeping pill he'd taken on the flight and his voice was clearly weak during the first few numbers. During a guitar solo Ozzy walked off stage, found Sharon in the wings and told her he didn't feel well enough to finish the show. Predictably Sharon was unimpressed. He might be feeling ill but that wasn't sufficient excuse to quit midway through a show and disappoint thousands of fans. What's more the resulting bad publicity would only confirm what many critics were beginning to whisper: that although Ozzy was still a crowd pleaser he was now past his prime. Sharon might be Ozzy's wife, and hated to see him suffer, but she was also his manager and a hard-headed businesswoman with her eye on the bigger picture. As Ozzy recalled later: 'I wanted to walk off stage, but my wife was like, "Ozzy, fucking get back out there."'

Ozzy finished the show, but the entire experience had been a wake-up call for Sharon. She realized that other younger and fresher-sounding rock bands had established themselves during Ozzy's retirement. To avoid Ozzy being seen as part of the old guard – out of date and out of touch – she needed to work hard and fast. The nostalgia circuit was not for her. She had no intention of wheeling Ozzy out on constant 'greatest hits' tours. Nor was playing second or third fiddle on the bill to supposedly bigger acts acceptable. She wanted people to accept Ozzy as a current star, playing new material. She had done it once before when she revamped his image after he left Black Sabbath and she had no doubts she could do it again. She would have her work cut out, that was for certain. But there was nothing Sharon enjoyed more than a challenge.

CHAPTER SEVEN

The Shape of Things to Come

❛ If you're a woman and you say no in business, they call you a bitch. If you say yes, you get shat on by everybody. So now I just do what I want and don't give a fuck what anybody else thinks. ❜

DESPITE HER GROWING REPUTATION in the world of music, many still made the mistake of judging Sharon by her appearance. She was a woman in the testosterone-charged world of rock and by now she was in her mid-forties in a business obsessed with youth. In addition, she still looked and dressed like a suburban housewife. Sharon's weight remained a problem to her. Periodically she would attempt to diet, but with limited success, the result being that she had gained a couple of pounds every year. Unhappy with her appearance she kept her hair short and neat and still took refuge in long shapeless skirts and blouses. All in all it gave the impression of a woman who wouldn't say boo to a goose. So in 1996, when the organizers of the fashionable travelling rock festival Lollapalooza turned her down when she approached them about the possibility of Ozzy appearing on the bill, they thought they would hear no more of her.

But the rejection gave Sharon a jolt. After Donington she knew she would have to work hard to change Ozzy's image; she just hadn't realized quite how hard. But slinking away with her tail between her legs after being rejected by Lollapalooza was not her style. As Sharon recalled: 'They laughed at the idea. They all thought Ozzy was so uncool. So I thought: "Right, I'll organize my own fucking festival."'

Sharon had never organized a festival before in her life, but she wasn't going to let a little thing like that put her off. She set about her task with breathtaking speed, working day and night. Frequently Ozzy woke in the small hours to find Sharon missing. Sleepily he would stumble from room to room only to find a light shining from under the door of their study. Inside he would find Sharon busily making notes and taking phone calls from around the world. She had been in the business long enough to have contacts in every single strand of the rock world. She called in a few favours, sought some advice and, most important of all, she stood no nonsense. It wasn't long before she had booked up some of the best heavy-metal music talent around – sixteen bands in all agreed to play, including Slayer, Neurosis, Biohazard, Prong, Fear Factory and Danzig. And of course topping the bill would be Ozzy.

Sharon realized that in order for the festival to stand apart from other rock events, it needed to establish its own identity. So as well as music there would be side stalls and shows. And as well as the usual stands offering beer, hot dogs and merchandise, there would be tents offering tattoos and body piercing. The name – an inspired choice – would be Ozzfest. The first show went ahead in Phoenix, Arizona on 14 September

1996 and was a sell-out. Sharon announced a second show later that year in Los Angeles and that too sold out.

Sharon had recently made a return to artist management, signing up hard-rock band Coal Chamber – the first new act she had taken on for several years. But Ozzfest gave her a new identity. Although Ozzy was a big part of it, the festival was undoubtedly Sharon's baby and she relished the opportunity it gave her. She had never sought fame; happy to let Ozzy take the limelight and hide away in the background. But Ozzfest was different. It meant she could still stay relatively anonymous to the outside world, but well and truly establish herself as a force to be reckoned with in the music business. And slowly but surely, people began to sit up and take notice.

Inspired by her success, the following year Sharon set about putting together Ozzfest 2. The first show had been a hard act to follow, but she pulled it off, historically reuniting Black Sabbath and ending the show with a set from Ozzy, Tony Iommi and 'Geezer' Butler. This time Ozzfest played twenty-two shows across America – the second highest-grossing tour in the States that year. It made Sharon realize it was time to make the States their home once more. As pop commentator Rick Sky explained: 'Ozzy's not really a musical great, he's an old-fashioned show-man. Sharon realized that his natural home would be America where they liked heavy metal and that vaudeville show. Normally in rock-and-roll once you've passed twenty-five you're a bit too old, but she really regenerated his career.'

Sharon and Ozzy sold their luxury mansion in Chalfont St Peter and bought a slightly smaller place just a couple of miles away, which would act as their holiday home. The money they saved would go on buying a bigger place in Los Angeles. Sharon was unsentimental about the move. She had spent more than half her life criss-crossing backwards and forwards between America and Britain and this was just one more move. As much as she had liked their house she still felt rootless – a result of her severed family ties in Britain. And Ozzy, for all his pride in being British, was still most at home on the road. Besides which, he trusted Sharon's judgement. If she felt they would be better placed in the States then he was happy to go along with it. As he explained: 'When it comes to the merchandising and financial side of Ozzy – the business decisions – I have complete and utter faith in my wife. Sometimes she's wrong, but most times she's right.'

What really made up Sharon's mind was that the children were also unsettled at school. Aimee had left boarding school and had been attending a local girls' school with Kelly, but both had been suspended, according to Kelly, after Aimee swore on the coach during a school trip. Sharon was furious and rang the headmistress immediately. Recalls Kelly: 'She said: "You're suspending my daughters because one swore and the other wouldn't tell on her own sister? What sort of morals do you have?" We never went back. My mum made the head cry.'

With the first two Ozzfests Sharon had been shrewd in her organization. What was important, she felt, was establishing the show as a credible and regular event and re-establishing Ozzy as a top-of-the bill artist. Making money, she decided, would have to wait until later. It was important to keep ticket prices down so fans would feel that they were getting value for money. She also chose to pay the performing bands well so they would want to appear again. Ozzy didn't even receive as much as many of the less famous singers, but as Sharon explained to her bemused husband, it really didn't matter – what she was building was a brand and in the long run that would pay off.

By 1998 Sharon's plan already seemed to be starting to work. Ozzfest 3 was booked to appear at thirty different venues over the summer, with Ozzy headlining alongside bands such as Motörhead, Megadeth, Limp Bizkit, Incubus and Tool. Many were rising stars and all were desperate to play alongside Ozzy. As Gary Bongiovanni, Editor-in-Chief of the American concert-business trade publication *Pollstar*, explained: 'Ozzfest was a brilliant move because the tour connects Ozzy to fans who are into younger nu-metal and hard-rock bands.' Just a few years previously Ozzy had been in severe danger of becoming a bloated pantomime artist, a mere shadow of his former self, but already Sharon had achieved her goal in making him fashionable again.

Sharon began 1999 by organizing a Black Sabbath reunion tour. There seemed to be huge demand from the fans and the band were friendly enough by now to make it work. The planning required several trips to New York, which Sharon would often undertake alone, but in April, growing tired of their separations, she booked Ozzy a ticket too. They would stay for a week, and when the business meetings were over they'd make a holiday of it – do a bit of sightseeing, catch some movies and visit their favourite bars, restaurants and shops. For the hotel Sharon had chosen an old favourite: the opulent St Regis Hotel on 55th Street, off Fifth Avenue.

After a week of pampering Sharon was in a good mood: the business meetings had gone well and she and Ozzy had spent some much-needed quality time together. Smiling, she told Ozzy to put his feet up and have a lie on the bed watching MTV while she packed. Ozzy had just started to nod off when a piercing scream jolted him from his slumbers. It was Sharon, cursing and yelling as she threw piles of clothes around the room. Ozzy jumped up in a panic, assuming that, as was often the case, the fury was aimed at him. A few minutes later Sharon calmed down enough to explain the reason for her outburst: £70,000 of jewellery had gone missing. The jewels were the bulk of her prized collection that she had built up over almost twenty years.

Someone must have got into their room while they were out and taken them, Sharon concluded. She shot out of the door and headed straight for the lifts and down to the lobby, demanding to see the hotel manager. Flustered, he ushered her into his office where it quickly became apparent that Sharon would not be appeased. When he told her he would do everything he could to help her find the jewels, but that it might take some time, she jumped up, ran back to the room and immediately phoned the police. With such a large theft on their hands the officer who took the call swung straight into action. Sharon and Ozzy had to leave for the airport, but the officer took a statement from them over the phone and promised that he would send someone down to the hotel within an hour. Sharon flew back to Beverly Hills feeling aggrieved, but satisfied that someone was now taking the case seriously.

When they arrived home she asked Ozzy to order in some food while she unpacked. As tempting as it was to leave the cases in the hall, she had a busy week ahead of her and knew it was best to get the task done now. As she sorted the clothes out into different piles Sharon reached the bottom of her case, where she had packed her shoes. She carefully lifted them out one by one, returning them to their boxes in the wardrobe. But when she lifted out the final pair her jaw dropped. There, tucked away in the bottom of the case, underneath her final pair of stilettos, were the missing jewels. Sharon couldn't believe it. Suddenly it all came back to her. She had hidden them there for safekeeping a couple of days earlier and had forgotten all about it. Shame-faced she slunk downstairs to confess all to Ozzy, before picking up the phone to call the manager of the St Regis Hotel to apologize for the mistake. Finally she made an embarrassed call to the New York police department, explaining how the jewellery had suddenly turned up. 'When they got back to Beverly Hills, Sharon Osbourne found the jewellery in the bottom of her luggage and called to apologize,' explained police spokesman Joseph Capitolo. 'They apparently forgot where they left the jewellery before they made the report.' Sharon may have had one of the sharpest brains in the music business, but at home, it seemed, chaos still reigned.

On her return to the States Sharon set about arranging that summer's Ozzfest – the festival was by now a must-attend gig for all self-respecting American rock fans, as well as bands. Fiercely protective of her creation, Sharon made sure that no one ever imagined they were bigger than Ozzfest itself. When the tour rolled in to New York in June, Sharon became so annoyed when Limp Bizkit frontman Fred Durst's set went on longer than anticipated that she took drastic action. She turned off the electricity, shutting down his microphone and the band's guitars. As a giggling Sharon later recalled: 'It was a big, lovely lever with a great big handle. It was even encased in red plastic. So I pulled it. The entire place went black. Pitch black everywhere. And it was silent for a moment. And then I ran!'

The incident summed up Sharon's complex personality perfectly. As the respected organizer of the entire Ozzfest tour she was entirely at ease handling top-level business meetings with promoters and executives. Polite and well-spoken and with a light, almost girlish voice, she would put her case across and then firmly stick to her guns. On the tour, handling the bands and singers, it was a different Sharon. Her language was frequently peppered with expletives. And if the singers annoyed her, as Fred Durst had done, she was not averse to the most impulsive and childish behaviour. At home her family saw yet another side to her – the kind-hearted and caring mum; eccentric by many families' standards, but still utterly devoted to her children.

The by-product of Ozzfest's success was that the tour was now making money, the likes of which Sharon and Ozzy had never earned before in their lives. Ozzy had always sold records, but this was something different. In the summer of 1999 Ozzfest 4 grossed £14 million. Far from having to persuade top-name bands to appear, Sharon was now fielding calls from desperate managers, all eager to get their acts on her bill. When asked how she succeeded in getting the various bands and managers to abide by what she said, Sharon summed it up simply: 'By having a foul mouth and not taking their abuse and being a rock. I mean, you have to be made of iron.' Those who crossed her inevitably regretted it, for her temper was by now legendary. As Kelly remembered in the second series of *The Osbournes*, a member of the rock group Motörhead ducked just in time as a furious Sharon hurled a heavy glass ashtray at his head after he upset her. Others regularly found themselves on the receiving end of her verbal onslaughts.

Still, Sharon's relationships with the groups she managed were unique in the business. She deliberately kept the number of acts in her stable small in order to give them her personal attention. Unlike other managers, who would run their bands from a distance, Sharon befriended hers and preferred to work only with people she knew, liked and respected. As Coal Chamber bassist Rayna Foss explained, Sharon would even invite bands to visit her at home in England. Coal Chamber themselves spent a memorable day in Buckinghamshire, riding motorbikes around the garden with Ozzy. Rayna said: 'She's a real force in the biz and she helps us a lot, makes contacts and all that. She liked us and we always respected her work. It's really great.'

In October 1999 Sharon announced she would be taking another new name under her wing, The Smashing Pumpkins. The popular rock band, led by charismatic singer Billy Corgan, were up-and-coming stars who had split with their former management team the previous year. They had undergone meetings with most of the major players in the industry, but had finally settled on hiring Sharon as their new manager. Sharon knew their decision would upset many in the rock business, but she didn't care. As far as she was concerned signing the band was a major coup. 'There's going to be some bruised egos, I'm sure,' she explained. 'I think Corgan wanted someone who would be hands-on, someone who doesn't have a whole roster of superstars, somebody who has been around a long time. Nobody has the history I do.'

With a Smashing Pumpkins album due out early in 2000 to be followed by a world tour, Sharon knew the start of the new millennium would be a busy time. But before it began she had one important thing to do. All her life Sharon had put other things first: her father, Ozzy, her children and her work. Now finally, at the age of forty-seven, she decided she must do something about herself – in particular her weight and binge eating. Sharon had been self-conscious about her size for some time. 'I knew what people were saying,' she recalled. 'It was always "Have you seen the wife? She's huge." Going to do business I knew as soon as I'd leave the room, they'd go "Fat cow."' Yet she had always hardened herself to it, telling herself it didn't matter. Her children weren't interested in her size and Ozzy loved her whatever she looked like. Whenever she had dieted in the past he had supported her, but always insisted that he found her attractive at any weight. He meant it and Sharon knew that, but now that wasn't enough.

She had already had to resort to Jack pushing her up the stairs. 'Literally when I went up the stairs at home Jack would be behind me holding my bum, helping me,' Sharon recalled. 'Now how sad was that?' But that wasn't all. In hot weather she now panicked about what to wear. In winter she would hide herself away under big jumpers, coats and scarves, but in the summer she would scour her wardrobe in desperation for something that would cover her up, yet also keep her cool. And so large was her stomach that she had developed sores underneath it. On top of that her health was beginning to suffer. She had become so heavy that she had constant backache and now needed steroid injections in her feet to ease the pain of supporting so much weight. 'I knew if I'd continued along the path I was on, I would have ended up in a wheelchair because I was so fat,' she later admitted. 'I just kept on getting bigger and bigger and more and more uncomfortable and I thought, "Oh God, I'm going to die."'

When she weighed herself the scales topped sixteen stone – excessive for her tiny five-foot-two-inch frame and the heaviest she had ever been in her life. Friends who knew about her eating problems had suggested she try therapy to get to the bottom of why she over-ate, but Sharon had always refused. 'I just went, "No, it's fine." It was the English way of saying, "I'm alright, there's nothing wrong."'

But now her body was telling her otherwise. Sharon knew diets wouldn't work for her; she had tried most of them over the years, but despite her best efforts she had a weakness for junk food that she just couldn't control. Given the choice of a fancy restaurant where she could order a salad and grilled chicken, or a McDonald's, Sharon would opt for the burger bar every time. In Los Angeles there were drive-in places on every corner and Sharon found them hard to resist. She loved fried food and, never a fan of the kitchen, she frequently relied on takeaways.

What finally prompted her decision to do something about her weight was an embarrassing meeting with music executives in New York. It took place in a hi-tech, minimalist office with tiny designer chairs. Sharon sat down and when the meeting ended she said thank you and made to get up. Unfortunately the meeting had gone on for two hours and during that time

Sharon had got warm and welded herself to her seat. 'And the bloody chair was stuck to me,' she recalls. 'I needed some help and one guy had to hold the back and I had a guy on each arm and they had to pull me off.' Sharon laughed it off, but inside she was mortified. It finally brought it home to her just how large she had become.

Sharon knew she needed drastic measures. She had recently read about a relatively new procedure that doctors in America were still perfecting and decided to give it a try. It was called gastric banding. During an operation a band would be inserted and put across the upper stomach, producing a small pouch, which could then only hold small amounts of food. Without telling Ozzy or her children, Sharon booked herself in. When she arrived home that evening and revealed what she had done, the family were furious, feeling that Sharon had put her health at risk simply to be slimmer. Sharon had always tried to bring up her children not to feel self-conscious about their weight and body size. Since they had returned to the States she had sensed the pressure to be slim – particularly on the two girls – but had always urged them to feel happy in their own skin. As a result they were baffled by their mother's actions. But Sharon had no doubt she had done the right thing. After just a few days in bed she was up and about as normal, eating the same foods but much smaller amounts. It meant that she initially felt hungry most of the time, but as the weeks passed her body adapted and the hunger pangs disappeared. As Sharon said, jubilantly: 'Finally something had controlled my eating.'

As the old millennium drew to a close, Sharon received a phone call from her brother breaking the news that her mother had died. A heavy smoker, Hope had been ill for some time with lung cancer. Sharon had not been to see her before her death, but had no regrets. 'It's not like I did the Irish jig when she died, I was just, "Oh really", the same way she was with me,' she explained. For Aimee and Kelly, who were so close to their own mother, it was unfathomable that a mother and daughter could have had such a poor relationship, but Sharon didn't see it as being hard-hearted or vindictive. She was simply being honest. When Sharon had been a young woman needing her mother's help and guidance as she made her way in the world, Hope had turned her away. Suddenly to pretend that all was well between them seemed hypocritical to Sharon. For that reason she decided against attending Hope's funeral. She couldn't feign heartache when she didn't feel it, and she certainly didn't want to have to encounter her father again if she could avoid it.

Sharon and Ozzy decided to see in the new millennium at their home in Buckinghamshire. Although Ozzy had successfully stayed off alcohol for five years, he had slipped again recently. Sharon was aware of it, but Ozzy did his best to hide it from her. Paranoid about newspaper reports of a 'millennium bug', Ozzy had convinced himself that his local supermarkets and off-licences would be closed down. As a precaution he had taken to buying huge quantities of vodka and burying it in the garden. To enable him to carry out his covert operation while Sharon was asleep he installed huge floodlights, which the neighbours, understandably, complained about. The story made the local papers when Ozzy insisted that the reason for the lights was that he found it difficult to sleep at night and liked to unwind with a little late-night gardening. On millennium night, however, it didn't take Sharon long to sniff out Ozzy's game as he periodically disappeared into the garden, returning later with a glazed smile on his face. As Ozzy recalled: 'After a while Sharon said, "Oi, you're drunk and where's all this effing vodka coming from?"'

At the start of 2000 Sharon decided to concentrate her efforts on managing The Smashing Pumpkins. Ozzfest 2000 was a few months away and she was relishing the opportunity to promote a new band. Sharon had high hopes for them and set to work. In spite of that, however, the partnership was not to last for very long. In March, after just three months in charge, Sharon quit via a legendary press statement. 'I must resign due to medical reasons,' it began. 'Billy Corgan is making me sick.' Afterwards, explaining the flash of her famous fiery temper, she said: 'I shouldn't have said it, but I like to be honest and after all these years I can't be bothered being politically correct.'

Sharon had no worries about the fall-out. She had grown up watching her father speak his mind and while she didn't take her business techniques to the same extreme, she was more than capable of standing her ground. She had been that way since she was a young woman and now she was older she was confident enough not to worry about the consequences. Besides, the way she saw it she had bigger fish to fry. She had learnt a lot during her time in the music business and had long since come to the conclusion that she could put her knowledge to even greater use by setting up her own record label. Now seemed the perfect time; it would complete the picture. Not only would she manage bands and organize their tours, but she would also be able to control the equally lucrative recording contracts. It would not be difficult – Sharon had the same passion for music she'd had as a teenager. Aged forty-seven, she still loved to spend her evenings at the hippest rock venues, checking out the latest bands. What's more, her children were teenagers now, shared her love of rock and kept her constantly up to date with changing trends.

Calling her label Divine Recordings, Sharon hired a suite of offices in West Hollywood. She obviously had instant access to the live recordings made at Ozzfest every year and some of Black Sabbath's back catalogue, but that wasn't enough for Sharon. What had always excited her about the music business was fresh, raw talent. She would use her new label, she decided, to sign up new bands. Her first signing was an up-and-coming Canadian heavy rock outfit called Slaves on Dope. They had recently moved to Los Angeles and Sharon had caught their debut twenty-five-minute set at a rock bar called the Opium Den in Hollywood in January. Word had spread quickly of the band's potential and Sharon wasn't the only scout there that night, but Slaves on Dope had no doubt that Sharon was the right person to steer their careers. Jason Rockman, the group's lead singer, explained: 'We had a chance at a whole bunch of other labels, but when Sharon came around to see us we dropped the other offers, because we knew she had a track record of breaking bands.'

The onset of summer saw another Ozzfest and Sharon booked up a twenty-nine-date tour that would keep them on the road for several months. Featuring Ozzy and nineteen other rock bands, Sharon could allow herself a wry smile, for Lollapalooza, the festival that had rejected Ozzy back in 1996 and prompted her to set up her own show, was no more. Ozzfest was the festival of the summer now. There were no other contenders and that was all down to her. Yet she knew from bitter experience that the more successful you were, the more you had to watch your back. Just before the tour began Sharon discovered that a merchandising company was advertising to record companies that, for a generous fee, it would promote new bands at Ozzfest. Sharon's view was that it was unethical to go inside someone else's tour and promote a band without permission. In a rage she drove down to the company's offices, walked in and trashed the place. 'I was so pissed off. I just went fucking mad,' she recalls. 'There were all these fucking computers that I threw and I kicked. But the joke was I left my car keys in there and I couldn't leave because they had my keys!' Sharon caught a cab home and the very next day a courier knocked on the door delivering a package from the merchandising company, which contained her car keys, a large bunch of flowers, and a note to say they were sorry. Sharon felt genuinely contrite about her behaviour, but sent them nothing to compensate for the damage or to indicate her regret. 'You never show weakness,' she explained afterwards.

Taking along the children and their nanny – a six-foot, goatee-bearded man named Dave – Sharon attended every date of Ozzfest, spending her days shuttling backwards and forwards between the main stage and the second stage in order to catch as many bands as she could. At one show in Boston though, Sharon wondered if her age had finally caught up with her. As she wandered through the black-clad crowd a scruffy group of teenage boys with straggly dreadlocked hair and pierced noses started to giggle. 'Hey, Sharon!' one called out. Not by nature timid Sharon had no fear of a group of teenage rebels, so she took a deep breath and turned round, ready to give the gang a piece of her mind. She needn't have worried. Before she even had chance to speak the boys' faces broke into huge smiles. 'Hey, Sharon! You fucking rock. This is the best fucking tour in the world! Rock on!' he continued. The boys all howled in agreement, saluting her with the traditional rock sign of the forefinger and small finger. Sharon grinned back and waved. But it was not enough for the boys. One of them broke free of his friends, ran over and insisted on a hug. Sharon obliged, but when he asked for an autograph, she felt enough was enough. As flattered as she was, she wasn't yet ready to cope with the attention on this scale. 'I'm not a performer. I'd just feel ridiculous,' she told him.

But there was no doubting Sharon's growing status on the tour. More earth mother than rock chick, she was every band's first port of call whenever anything went wrong. A singer suffering from bronchitis was assessed by Sharon and then sent to the Ozzfest in-house doctor for treatment. Established artists would drop by the catering hall simply for a chat, while younger acts would wander up and ask for advice. At one show a shaven-headed musician was even dispatched to give Sharon a hand-written note from his mother, thanking her for taking her son on the tour. For there was no doubt now what a difference the festival made to bands. A spot at Ozzfest could propel a group to gold or platinum status within a matter of months.

When the artists weren't demanding her attention, Sharon was doing her best to keep a close eye on Aimee, Kelly and Jack. As young children they had looked almost angelic, with neat hair and cherubic smiles, the girls in pretty dresses and Jack frequently in smart trousers and waistcoat. But they were teenagers now and acted and dressed accordingly. It was partly typical teenage rebellion and partly a reaction to being in the States. The children had felt out of place ever since moving back to Los Angeles and had not settled well. Jack had found the whole experience so stressful he had been in therapy since he was twelve and had recently been diagnosed with depression. Kelly felt uncomfortable in an environment where her classmates considered her fat merely because she didn't watch her figure and count calories in the obsessive way that they did. 'In England it was uniform and rules, in America it was girls in Dolce and Gabbana clothes on cellphones,' she recalled.

With none of them having any great love of school they certainly made the most of it when they were allowed off the leash for Ozzfest. While (according to Sharon) an embarrassed seventeen-year-old Aimee wandered around saying that her real father was a builder, Kelly was wreaking havoc fighting constantly with Dave the nanny, even biting him when she disagreed with his orders. She had grown up fast and at sixteen was wise beyond her years. As she explained: 'I've had a different upbringing, seen things children should never see. Like being backstage at rock shows when you're five years old, seeing people doing drugs. People think that if you're rich and famous, you have no problems. Being rich and famous is my biggest problem.' Meanwhile Jack, at fourteen, had become obsessed with the stranger elements of the tour and was more than happy to be the guinea pig for performance artist the Reverend B. Dangerous, whose finale featured him pushing a drill up his nose. On one occasion Sharon found the Reverend trying to ease a plastic spoon two inches up Jack's left nostril, only stopping when Jack started to gag. Most mothers would have been aghast at such a sight, but Sharon, as ever, seemed unfazed by the whole thing. 'My strategy is not to react, because if I react, he'll only keep doing it,' she explained. On this occasion, however, it only seemed to propel Jack to greater acts of rebellion and when he later had his head shaved on stage by Methods of Mayhem, she could no longer hold back. 'What happened to my baby boy?' she screeched. 'You look like a convict!' It was an unorthodox way for them all to live, but it was the only way of life any of them knew. There were boundaries Sharon would not allow them to cross – she and Ozzy lectured them constantly about drugs – but she was now prepared to cut them a little more slack in other ways, turning a blind eye to their bad language and the occasional drink.

As much as Sharon enjoyed the day-to-day problem-solving with the bands and the banter with her children, there was one part of the show that still gave her goose pimples. At 9.45 p.m., with the lights down and dry ice pumping out, Ozzy would take to the stage, wearing black tracksuit bottoms with silver thunderbolts down the sides and a black T-shirt. Everyone in the crowd, from sixteen to fifty years old, would chant his name. For Sharon it was the one moment in the day when she could take off her tour-promoter hat and simply be the loyal wife waiting in the wings. Her relationship with Ozzy had, if anything, grown stronger over the years. Although they were tied up with work and parenting these days, he was still her best friend – the one man in the world that could make her laugh. She still respected and admired him, and relished every second of seeing him on stage. 'It makes me so proud,' she admitted. 'They just love him so much. It makes everything worth it.'

When the tour ended Sharon was due a well-earned rest, but as was increasingly becoming the case there was simply no time. She had parted company with Coal Chamber, but she and Ozzy had kept in touch with former Black Sabbath guitarist Tony Iommi after the Black Sabbath reunion concerts, and when Tony mentioned he was keen to start work on his first solo album, Sharon offered to put it out on her label. The record was due for release in October and Sharon found herself tied up for weeks, in the studio and talking to distributors, TV companies and record stores.

Throughout the summer friends and colleagues had slowly begun to notice a change in Sharon. Her banding operation had proved a great success and the weight had fallen off at the steady rate of two or three pounds a week. By the early autumn of 2000 she was down to less than nine stone, having shed almost half of her body weight. The downside was that she had been left with areas of flabby skin, most noticeably on her stomach. 'My stomach was like a little kangaroo,' she admitted. 'I used to have to lift it up to wash underneath. And I had *National Geographic* boobies.' Her face, which previously had been plump, was now looking a little lined. She was not naturally vain and had always mocked women who felt the need for cosmetic surgery, but suddenly, with a slim figure, she found herself contemplating what had previously been the unthinkable. If she had gone through the effort of having her stomach banded and losing more than seven stone in weight, she decided she might as well finish what she had started and put the final touches to her new look.

After a lot of thought Sharon decided to start with a facelift. She asked around her friends and was given the name of a surgeon, Dr Leslie Stevens, who was based at the Lasky Clinic, just off Santa Monica Boulevard in Beverly Hills, not far from her home. Dr Stevens specialized in facelifts, breast lifts, liposuction, Botox and lip augmentation – in fact everything Sharon was considering. She arranged an initial appointment for a facelift and brow lift and went along full of excitement. But at her first consultation she was so horrified by the frank description of how her face would be cut and her skin pulled back, she almost walked out. When she eventually recovered she begged them to go ahead, but simply not tell her any more of the gruesome details. After surgery it took her two weeks to recover and she admitted that although delighted with the results, she had found the whole experience agonizing. 'If anybody says their facelift doesn't hurt they're lying,' she said afterwards. 'It was like I'd spent the night with an axe murderer. They take your ears off and put them back on! I didn't look for four days – I was petrified. Finally I thought "This is ridiculous" and I saw the difference immediately: I didn't have a double chin and I didn't have my jowls.' Sharon followed it up a few months later with liposuction work on her neck, arms and hips – where they removed eight pounds of fat – and also surgery on her stomach. 'I had this big flap of skin that hung over my crotch. Very sexy, let me tell you. So I had a tummy tuck and they took so much skin off they had to make a new belly button,' she explained.

Now slim, shapely and unlined, Sharon began to notice a huge difference in the way people treated her. For a long time her legendary temper had ensured that no one in the music business gave her anything less than 100 per cent respect – to her face at any rate. But suddenly she found that on planes and in the street she was attracting the attention of strangers – men who normally would not have given her the time of day. As Sharon explained: 'When you are big nobody holds a door open for you. When you're at the airport waiting for your case on the carousel, nobody wants to know and nobody wants to help. It's amazing. And then when you come in skinny and you put your boobies up a bit, it's like, "I'll get your case for you." I travel back and forth all the time and I always sit next to some businessman. I'd put my old slippers on and there was not a word. Nobody would even look my way in case they thought I would speak to them and then when I lost all the weight and had all my surgery it was, "Do you travel this way a lot?"'

Most women would have been flattered beyond belief by such flirtations, particularly had they received as little attention from men as Sharon over the years. Instead she merely raised a quizzical eyebrow at them and returned politely to her magazine. She was the same person now as she had been when she was 100 pounds heavier and found it vaguely ridiculous that men only seemed to want to know her now she was thinner. Such men did not impress Sharon. As she explained: 'I had seen the way people react to fat people. Somebody once said that it's more acceptable to be a drug addict than it is to be fat. And it's true.'

CHAPTER EIGHT

Mother Knows Best

❝ I made fun of the ladies who were nipped, tucked and pulled. That is, until I joined the club. Now I've got my membership, I'm not going to let it expire. ❞

WITH SHARON'S REPUTATION growing by the day and her figure becoming shapelier by the month, her confidence was riding high. Ozzy's singing career, once their main source of income, was now playing second fiddle to Sharon's growing music empire. Sharon, who knew how much money they had in their bank accounts to the penny, was already well aware how successful they had become, but when the couple debuted on the *Sunday Times* Rich List at the start of 2001, suddenly the whole world began to sit up and take note. Sharon and Ozzy were listed as sharing a joint fortune of an incredible £40 million. And what was more, Sharon had generated more than half of it. Ozzy was a big name and had sold more than 170 million records, but he had earned and lost his fortune several times before Sharon took a firm grip on his career. Instead the bulk of their fortune had been earned through Sharon's cash cow,

Ozzfest, with additional income from her artist-management activities and record label.

Such wealth left Sharon in the fortunate position of being able to turn down work she didn't feel was right. In early 2001 that meant declining several requests from some of the biggest names around. With her own music label, her own sell-out tour and a track record in artist management, stars such as veteran rock band Guns N' Roses and Courtney Love (Kurt Cobain's girlfriend) requested career guidance. Even Limp Bizkit's lead singer Fred Durst forgave Sharon for blacking him out on stage at Ozzfest and asked her for help. Sharon politely, but very firmly, said no to them all. 'It's just I've gotten old and my temper's gotten very bad,' she explained. 'And to be a personal manager – some clients don't like to hear the truth – so you have to tap dance and mollycoddle them.' She still had Ozzy and Ozzfest to manage and she wanted to be able to turn her hand to new projects as and when they arose. Besides, she needed some spare time for her visits to Dr Stevens . . .

Sharon had spent so much time with her surgeon by now that he had become a family friend and she trusted him implicitly. While some Hollywood wives came away from cosmetic surgery with faces that seemed stretched and unnatural, Dr Stevens had succeeded in transforming Sharon's features in the most subtle way possible. She looked young and fresh-faced, but there were no visible telltale signs of surgery whatsoever. Inspired, she returned again and again. She started the year with Botox injections to remove the frown lines on her forehead, and then a few weeks later followed them up with a leg lift. 'They literally pull your legs up like a stocking,' she explained. One form of treatment she refused to consider though was any enhancement to her lips. She had already tried it several years previously, when collagen injections were the latest trend, but stopped halfway through, finding it too painful. 'I had half a top lip done and I said, "I'm out of here,"' Sharon recalled. 'It was excruciatingly painful. I walked around with half a top lip done and it took about six weeks for it to get back to normal.'

Lips aside, Sharon continued on her quest for the perfect body. Once she had recovered from the work on her legs she returned for a bottom lift and implant. As she admitted later: 'One of my kids said, "No more, Mom. No more surgery." But it was too late. It was like opening Pandora's Box. Ozzy said anyone who gets one tattoo wants another one. I think plastic surgery is like tattoos. If you're happy with the results, then you push the button again and again.' Sharon had never looked back since the gastric-banding operation. Previous diets had required her to cut out junk food and eat fresh salad and veg-etables, but the gastric banding meant that she could still indulge herself with her favourite food – fried potatoes, burgers, chips, butter and milk shakes – as long as she kept the portions small.

The irony was that as Sharon's health and appearance were improving, Ozzy's seemed to be in decline. On 10 April 2001 his mother Lillian died. Although life on the road meant he had seen little of her for many years, they had remained close and Ozzy took her death very badly. Terrified that he might go to pieces completely he decided against attending her funeral. Sharon had left the decision to Ozzy, but also felt he was wise to stay away, while they attempted to deal with his various prob-lems. The couple had consulted the best doctors that money could buy in both Britain and America, but all had come to the same sad conclusion, that Ozzy's heavy use of drink and drugs over the decades had taken its toll. Doctors told him that the years of abuse had caused a chemical imbalance in his brain, which needed to be controlled with prescription drugs. In addi-tion he had begun to visit a psychiatrist on an almost daily basis, and he was taking further drugs to control his insecurity, depres-sion and insomnia. Physically he was now moving slowly, with a slight stoop and a shuffling gait. His hands were limp and shaky. His hearing was poor – the deafening music he played at concerts had damaged his eardrums – and at times he stammered and struggled to get his words out.

Yet thanks to Sharon's intuitive guidance, Ozzy was just as much in demand musically as ever before. There were continual Black Sabbath reunion tours and Sharon now had him back in the studio working on songs for a new album. Sharon also found time to work with family friend and *Wayne's World* director Penelope Spheeris on a new movie, *We Sold Our Souls to Rock 'n' Roll*, a fly-on-the-wall record of the previous year's Ozzfest. One film highlight showed a spirited public debate between Sharon and a preacher picketing a show, who informed her that her husband was 'a practising cannibal'. 'That's about the one thing Ozzy hasn't done,' Sharon retorted, deadpan.

In May Ozzfest 2001 took to the road. Ozzy was baffled by the way that it kept going, year after year. 'I keep saying to Sharon, "How long is it gonna go?" And she'll go, "We'll know when it's time to pull out." Every year it gets bigger and bigger, what else am I gonna do?' Ozzy and Black Sabbath were the headline band as usual, with some of the biggest names in rock appearing alongside them, including Slipknot, Linkin Park, Marilyn Manson, Tool, Black Label Society and Papa Roach. Also on the bill, on the support stage, was a new band by the name of Pure Rubbish. Sharon had seen them play a couple of times previously, and after their barnstorming performance at Ozzfest they became the latest signing to her Divine Recordings label. Sharon wasn't one for hanging around and by August their debut single 'Kiss of Death' was rush-released.

All the Osbourne children once more accompanied Sharon and Ozzy on the tour. Aimee, eighteen, and Kelly, seventeen, had now both dropped out of school and Sharon was finding it a struggle to make fifteen-year-old Jack attend lessons. None of them enjoyed the academic life. Aimee had suffered from depression in her mid-teens and also struggled with dyslexia, like her father. It had reached the point where school had become so overwhelming and upsetting for her that when she woke up one day and told her mother she just couldn't do it any more, Sharon immediately accepted her decision. Kelly too had encountered problems. Increasingly she had felt that the teachers simply didn't understand her and that, jealous of her lifestyle, they would penalize her whenever they could.

Sharon sympathized with their plight. For a while she had encouraged them to do their best, but in her heart she didn't feel an academic education was essential to get on in the world. 'My kids aren't scientists; they don't fit in. What are you gonna do? Force them because it's the thing to do, it's politically correct and I have to keep up with the neighbours because their kids are all at big colleges?' she explained. 'It's not like Kelly wants to be a botanist. They can all read and write perfectly and they're in the school of life.' Both Sharon and Ozzy had quit school when they were fifteen and while that was no longer legally allowed, Aimee and Kelly had only remained in education for as long as they must, until they were sixteen. Kelly was intent on a career in show business and Aimee, like her father, was desperate for her own music career, although her style was a world away from her father's heavy rock. She preferred a quieter, more reflective sound and was determined to make it on her own.

With Ozzfest the most successful summer rock tour in the world, Sharon was now able to indulge herself more and more in her favourite pastime . . . shopping. She had grown up enjoying the finer things in life, and the lesson she had learnt from her father at a very early age was that if you had money you spent it. In the past, she had treated herself to jewellery and beautiful furniture, rugs and ornaments for their homes; antiques were her weakness. She would also splash out on cars – often without telling Ozzy. On one occasion a vehicle was delivered to their house and when Ozzy asked the delivery driver what was happening, Sharon ran out and thanked him for buying it. 'I said: "I haven't bought you a car,"' recalls Ozzy. 'She said: "I did, but I thought you wouldn't mind." I said: "What about me having a car?" She said: "I've sent my BMW to be repaired; you can have that one." I said: "Who's the rock star around here?"'

The added joy of losing so much weight was that Sharon was able to indulge herself with a whole new wardrobe. Shopping when she was a size eighteen had not been much fun and there had been a limited choice, but now that she was a petite size eight she could take her pick from the rails. She had a good eye for fashion and very quickly developed her own distinctive style: sharp black trouser suits, fitted basque tops, tailored jackets and frock coats and black cashmere jumpers – all set off with stunning diamond jewellery. Sharon knew how to mix and match her wardrobe and within the space of a couple of years she had become so well known in the expensive boutiques along Rodeo Drive that she knew the shop assistants by name. Frequently she would take Kelly with her. Kelly loved shopping just as much as her mum and she was happy to be Sharon's partner in crime, hiding some of the bigger purchases from Ozzy. It wasn't that the family couldn't afford them, but coming from a humble background Ozzy had never shaken off a slight worry over spending. He was not in the least materialistic and could not see the fun in shopping for shopping's sake. To avoid alarming him Sharon and Kelly would hide the shopping bags in the back of the car, slowly taking a couple out every day so Ozzy wouldn't notice.

With money no object, that summer Sharon and Ozzy decided to make their biggest purchase yet – a stunning new

Mediterranean-style home in Beverly Hills. They sold their old place, moved into a rented house in Malibu and began to search for their dream property. It didn't take long to find. Costing £2 million, it sat high in the streets above Sunset Boulevard and was like something out of a Hollywood film. Sharon, Ozzy and the family had lived in the area for some time, but this house was something different. Here Sharon could live out her dreams. Inside was room after room. Downstairs were the large kitchen, sitting room, formal dining room, games room and Sharon's office, as well as two additional sitting rooms – one for Sharon and one for Ozzy. Upstairs was a gym, Sharon and Ozzy's en-suite bedroom, a two-room suite for Kelly, a large en-suite room for Jack and another for Aimee, several spare rooms and two bathrooms. Taking pride of place in the perfectly manicured back garden sat a landscaped swimming pool complete with rocks, a waterfall and slide. Elsewhere there was a secret hidden grotto, a jacuzzi and dozens of imposing statues.

With such a perfect home, Sharon decided it was finally time to attempt to become the perfect wife. While she had always been a devoted mum, domestic duties had never been high on her list of priorities. Her children could rarely persuade her to make a sandwich for them, let alone a hot meal. But now, with a beautiful new kitchen in place, Sharon decided it was time to put it to good use: she was finally going to learn how to cook. But if her family were expecting traditional dishes such as shepherd's pie or lasagne, they were in for a huge surprise. Having reached the age of forty-eight and never having served up a proper meal, Sharon decided it would be best to start slowly. 'And we had turkey dinosaurs with Bird's Eye potato waffles every night,' Kelly recalls. When the family complained about the lack of variety, Sharon simply went back to the freezer section of her local store and this time opted for something a little more exotic – turkey meatballs stuffed with garlic butter.

Unfortunately, having put them in the oven, Sharon promptly forgot about them, until smoke started billowing into the sitting room. The meatballs had split open in the heat and the butter had caught fire. As they called the fire brigade in a panic, Sharon put her pinny back in the drawer and, thrusting a pizza-delivery leaflet into their hands, firmly told the children the days of home cooking were well and truly over.

In September Sharon and Ozzy travelled to New York. It was a trip that would combine business and pleasure – a few meetings and lots of shopping. Their stay coincided with the devastating 9/11 attacks on the city. Sharon and Ozzy were staying in the Peninsula Hotel close to the World Trade Center. While they had never been in any imminent danger the events of that day affected them badly. They had watched the carnage unfold from the roof of their hotel and were so shaken by what they had witnessed that, when it seemed safe to go out, they went to a church across the road to gather their thoughts. When they got back the events of that day set Sharon thinking. While she had shed no tears over her mother's death and genuinely had no regrets about failing to make her peace with her before she died, things were different with her father. Don and Sharon had always shared a special bond when she was young and she had been devastated by their falling-out. As she explained: 'Being estranged from my father broke my heart. Even though I didn't respect him, felt betrayed by him . . . I still loved him. I'd still think to myself: "Maybe I will bump into my dad today."' After all those years of secretly hoping they would be reconciled, Sharon now knew there was no point leaving it to chance: it was down to her to do something about it.

But in the meantime it was back to work. In October 2001 Sharon oversaw the release of *Down to Earth*, Ozzy's first record for six years. Sharon had spent the intervening years concentrating on making Ozzfest a huge success. Now it was so well established she felt Ozzy could go back to basics. The album received rapturous reviews in the press and dominated the music headlines. Yet it was about to become overshadowed, as were most things in their lives, by the arrival of a television crew at their home . . .

Television was an area Sharon had wanted to break into for a long time. Ozzy had a wide and respectable fan base, but only a small percentage of the population listened to heavy rock and that was never going to change. Sharon had won him various bit-parts in movies, but she knew that television was the only real way to reach the masses. It was the only way to turn Ozzy from a cult rocker into an all-round entertainer. Coming from her variety background she had always felt that performers should be capable of turning their hands to most things. Ozzy had wit and charisma and was a one-off. His one-liners were hilarious and his approach to life was so off-the-wall that people who met him were captivated. She had no doubt he would be a success on television, it was simply a case of finding the right vehicle for his unique talents. She had made several attempts over the past ten years, spurred on by show-business friends who had convinced her that Ozzy and she were both made for television, but nothing had come of her efforts.

The first spark of a project occurred in their previous LA home. Sharon and Ozzy had lived next door to legendary 1950s crooner Pat Boone, and had struck up an unlikely friendship with the squeaky-clean singer. When a TV company got wind of this they thought it would make the ideal basis for a comedy series. Scriptwriters were dispatched to the Osbourne house in order to come up with a sitcom based on their life, but they soon realized that day-to-day life in the Osbourne household was far funnier than anything they could write themselves. Instead TV executives suggested a fly-on-the-wall documentary series charting everyday life at home with the Osbournes. Sharon agreed to a pilot episode, but when the TV company saw the hilarious footage they persuaded her to sign up for a full series. Sharon agreed a fee of £200,000 and for that a full-time TV crew would move in, setting up twelve cameras and staying with the family for five months, twenty-four hours a day. The only rules were that the bedroom and bathroom were out of bounds. What's more, eldest daughter Aimee, eighteen, would not be filmed. For a long while Aimee had felt the odd one out in her family – the normal one living amidst a bunch of eccentrics. She was desperate to make it on her own in the music business, without being associated with her famous father, and she was also by nature shy and reserved. She enjoyed her anonymity and felt that if she became part of *The Osbournes* she would be type-cast right away, before she had the chance to experience other things. Sharon was hurt and disappointed, but had no intention of forcing Aimee and instantly accepted her decision, so when the rest of the house all voted to take part, Aimee said she would move out. Sharon spoke to MTV about the problem and they agreed to provide a flat near by for Aimee to stay in so she would not become estranged from her family. Even so, on the day Aimee moved out Sharon felt sad. She had always been close to her first-born and she knew that she would miss her desperately.

Ozzy had been slightly bemused by the arrival of the TV crew, but he had gone along with Sharon's idea without much resist-ance. He had long since accepted Sharon as the boss, and when she had made her mind up about something it was fairly difficult to resist. Besides, Ozzy had other things on his mind – his first solo tour for seven years. As a mark of respect to the thousands of people who had lost their lives in the 9/11 outrage, Sharon had hastily changed the name of the tour from 'Black Christmas' to 'Merry Mayhem', and had also arranged a World Trade Center benefit show at the Meadowlands Stadium in New Jersey on 23 December. The couple also visited Ground Zero, where

Ozzy was presented with an iron cross made out of steel from the World Trade Center by New York police and firefighters. The couple had been moved by the tragedy, so much so that Sharon set up a special Ozz Bless America booth at every show, where proceeds from the merchandise sold would go directly to the fund set up for firefighters and their families.

With thoughts of 9/11 in her head once more, Sharon realized she could ignore her family problems no longer. She had been brooding about the situation with her father since September. When Ozzy received a phone call from her brother David informing him that Don was in a bad way, she knew it was finally time to end their feud. Sharon had fallen out with David at the same time as she had become estranged from her father, but her brother had called her out of the blue a few years previously and asked if they could make up. Things had been initially tense and awkward, but they had both persevered and kept loosely in touch. Now David was calling to break the bad news that Don not only had a bad heart, but he was also suffering from Alzheimer's and his memory was fading. He had given Ozzy the news and, conscious of the ongoing feud between Sharon and Don, had asked him not to tell her. But Ozzy chose to anyway. He knew that despite being angry with Don, Sharon still loved her father and would want to see him if he was ill. Sharon recalls: 'My husband said to me: "Go see him before he's totally wiped clean." I did.'

David arranged a meeting for afternoon tea at the Four Seasons Hotel in LA and a nervous Sharon turned up to meet the man she had only seen twice in the last twenty years. As those occasions had been marred by Sharon's attempts to scald Meredith with hot soup and to run both Don and Meredith down, understandably he was a little wary of her motives. 'I half expected some sort of scam or showdown,' he admitted later. 'But when I got there I realized she was nervous too, and that she didn't really know what to expect from this meeting either.' After a few minutes of polite conversation the years rolled away and soon Sharon and Don were laughing and chatting together like it was old times. At the end of the tea they hugged each other tight and agreed not to talk about the past, but to enjoy their remaining time together. Don was seventy-four and Sharon felt they had wasted enough years feuding. Don had never met his three grandchildren, and Sharon promised that now they had made up, they would never fall out again. 'Just because I'm a Nazi at work, I know it doesn't mean I have to be like that at home,' she explained.

Sharon left the meeting with her father on a huge high and rushed home excitedly to tell Ozzy her news. Overnight she went from not speaking to Don for twenty years to phoning him every other day. And just a couple of weeks later she invited him round to the house for dinner to see Ozzy again and meet his grandchildren. As they sat outside in the garden eating by candlelight, they laughed and joked and caught up on each other's lives.

At the start of 2002 Sharon and Ozzy headed abroad with Ozzy's 'Merry Mayhem' tour. Kelly went with them, but Jack stayed behind. Since the age of fourteen Jack had longed to follow in his mother's footsteps, spending every spare moment in clubs checking out new bands, advising his mum on the latest up-and-coming acts that might be worth signing up to her record label. Jack had also spent some time working as a scout for Epic Records, and now, having just set up a record label of his own, he wanted to concentrate even more on his work.

The 'Merry Mayhem' tour took in Japan, Korea, Canada, Germany and a first-ever stop in Alaska. But if the frozen North was going crazy for the Prince of Darkness, it was nothing compared to what was happening back in the States. On 5 March the first episode of *The Osbournes* premiered on MTV. The opening show, filmed the previous autumn, showed them moving into their new house. The décor was clearly fabulous, but it soon became clear that Sharon and Ozzy were intent on imposing their own original style on the place. Over the arched front doors they had erected crucifix spyholes, along with a huge demonic gargoyle. They were seen unpacking boxes clearly labelled 'pots and pans', 'linen', 'devil heads', 'dead things'. Among the chintz curtains and sofas – Sharon's choices – were crucifix door handles and paintings of Sodom and Gomorrah. It was an extraordinary sight.

The show was an instant hit, developing an early cult following. But word of mouth spread and it was soon pulling in more than six million viewers an episode – the highest rated show in the channel's twenty-year history. A real-life cross between *The Simpsons*, *The Beverly Hillbillies* and *The Addams Family*, America had never seen anything quite like it before. With the bad language – and there was plenty of it – bleeped out, it appealed across the board, from rebellious teenagers to middle-aged rockers to mums and dads and even grandparents. Everyone was mesmerized by the sight of Ozzy padding around the house in tracksuit bottoms, with his hair tied back in a ponytail, Kelly and Jack breaking every rule in the house and Sharon shouting, screeching and swearing in the background as she tried to keep some sort of order amidst the mayhem. A unique combination of eccentricity, celebrity and lack of self-consciousness made the show compulsive viewing. Music journalist Rick Sky summed up the programme's success: 'The fascination of the show is Ozzy. He's a great English eccentric – he's a real character and he's very funny. But he's too busy clowning around to have any business sense and the show would not have come off without Sharon. Together they're a wonderful combination – someone with great business sense meets someone with a great talent to entertain.'

When Sharon and Ozzy returned to the States in the spring, following the end of the 'Merry Mayhem' tour, Sharon paid yet another visit to her old friend Dr Leslie Stevens. This time it was for more Botox and breast surgery. As Sharon bluntly put it: 'My nipples were pointing south and I wanted them to point north.' The operation took Sharon's expenditure on surgery to more than £200,000, but she had no regrets. 'It was worth every last penny. I love cosmetic surgery,' she explained. 'For me, if something bothers you about your appearance, just get it changed. If you're lucky enough to be in a position to afford it, if it makes you feel better about yourself, go for it. You're not hurting anyone.'

After a quick visit to a private dentist to have her teeth whitened, the transformation of Sharon Osbourne was almost complete. She had a wardrobe to die for, enviable cheekbones and a stunning figure. And to add the finishing touch, she now had a new hairstyle. During the years she was overweight, Sharon had tended to keep her hair short and neat, but her new-found interest in her appearance had given her the confidence to experiment. She had begun to grow her hair the previous year and had it layered with a long, choppy fringe, and now her stylist had persuaded her to ditch her natural mousey brown colour in favour of a rich red auburn rinse, giving her hair a glossy warm sheen. When she appeared at Ozzy's side in April as he received his own star on Hollywood's prestigious Walk of Fame, the effect was stunning. The photographers took pictures of Ozzy, naturally, it was his big day and an indication of just how respected he had become, but at the same time they also fought to get Sharon into their shots too. Now forty-nine years old she looked a decade younger in a stylish pale pink frock coat, black trousers and shirt and diamond hoop earrings.

Approaching her landmark half-century it seemed that Sharon had finally beaten the demons that had seen her taking refuge in binge eating all her adult life. Yet only her family knew that behind the slim hips there was a different story. Sharon's bulimia was still there and at times of stress she still reached for the biscuit tin and ate and ate until she was sick. She had hoped the gastric band might have helped cure her and when she lost all her excess weight she thought her new shape would do it, but to her disappointment nothing seemed to work. Her family hated it, but Sharon refused to discuss it, burying away her thoughts and praying that one day it might just go away of its own accord. She had tackled a great many of her demons, but this was one that for now was going to have to wait.

With *The Osbournes* a hit on television, Sharon found to her surprise that she, Kelly and Jack were in almost as much demand as Ozzy. It had taken just ten weeks for their lives to change completely. They were now huge television stars, with the world's media desperate to interview them and the general public equally as anxious for autographs in the street. Stylists started to send trucks full of free designer clothes in the hopes they would wear them on screen. Mobile-phone companies were in touch offering their services, also for free. For Sharon, who had worked hard all her life for everything she owned, it took some adjusting to and at times she felt awkward. 'They don't charge you for anything, not even hotel rooms,' she explained. 'It's unbelievable. Now we go to pay the bill at a restaurant and they're like "Why?" I never realized the power of TV.' Yet at the same time Sharon was flattered and when total strangers approached her in the street to say how much they loved her family, she revelled in the attention: 'It makes me feel great. I'm like, "Yes, so do I, thank you!"'

Inspired by the popularity of her whole family rather than just Ozzy, Sharon decided to strike while the iron was hot and launch Kelly into the world of pop. Kelly, like her sister Aimee, had wanted to follow her father into the music business for some time. Unlike Aimee – who wanted to carve her own way with a different type of music – Kelly didn't mind too much what she did. A few months earlier Sharon had asked Aimee if she would like to record a version of Madonna's 1986 chart-topper 'Papa Don't Preach', but Aimee had turned her down. (Aimee's version is that she suggested to Ozzy that Kelly should sing it.) So Sharon decided to help Kelly record the song instead. It was an amusing choice, considering Kelly spent most of her time in *The Osbournes* telling her father to let her live her own life. Sharon was convinced the record-buying public would love the irony. Keeping things in the family, Sharon asked Jack to produce it. The song would appear on the upcoming sound-track for *The Osbournes* and would eventually be released as a solo single.

On 26 May 2002 *The Osbournes* transferred to Britain. News had spread from the States and when it arrived, more than 500,000 viewers tuned in to MTV to watch the opening episode – a huge number for a satellite show and beating ITV1 in homes that had digital, cable or satellite TV. As Sharon observed shrewdly: 'I knew it would be big. Ozzy is not the kind of guy who comes home carrying his briefcase at the end of a hard day's work.' But surprisingly, it was not Ozzy but Sharon who was emerging as the star of the show. Most people knew a lit-tle about the singer and his reputation as a man who had bitten the head off a bat and a dove, but few knew anything about his diminutive wife. With a ready smile and perfectly coiffured hair, on first appearances Sharon seemed every inch the typical, demure LA housewife. But within just a few shows the reality became clear. In one episode entitled 'Won't You Be My Neighbour?', Sharon goes to war with neighbours who she says are keeping her awake by playing loud music and acoustic gui-tar until the small hours of the morning. It is an ironic accusation from a woman whose husband made his living blasting out loud rock music, but what makes it hilarious viewing is the way Sharon handles the situation. As Kelly asks: 'You went over there and asked them to quieten down and they didn't?' Sharon replies with a wicked grin: 'No, I didn't quite say it like that. I said, "Shut the fuck up you middle-aged something or others."' Viewers then see the full exchange, with Sharon taunting one of the neighbours: 'Darling, the wicked witch has nothing on me; you're living next door to the neighbour from hell. Come on big boy, come here. Come on cocky little Englishman, come down here little rich boy. Live off Daddy's money do you?' Sharon then invites them round to discuss the problem the following day, telling Kelly that when one of them appears she intends to 'hold him down and piss on his head'. Even Kelly is shocked, telling Sharon: 'That's a bit much, Mum'. When the same thing happens the next night Sharon responds by hurling bagels and a ham into the neighbour's garden, at which point the police are called. In another episode Sharon takes a whisky bottle into the bathroom and pretends to urinate into it to stop the children and their friends from drinking.

If viewers are sometimes left wondering whether Sharon's more outrageous stunts are simply for the benefit of the television cameras, Jack is able to confirm otherwise. In an interview given to promote the show he revealed that he was only thirteen when Sharon first flashed at one of his friends as they sat in the kitchen eating dinner one evening. 'My mum comes in, lifts up her shirt and goes, "Ryan, do you think I'm sexy?"' Jack recalled. 'It wasn't a full-on flash. She still had her bra on. And I was like, "Oh my tucking [sic] God."' The show also gave viewers a fascinating insight into Sharon's unorthodox way of parenting. At one point she calls a family meeting, upset at the fact that seventeen-year-old Kelly and fifteen-year-old Jack, still at school at the time, are out partying on weekdays until 2 a.m. But when she complains that the family has no structure to its life, Kelly points out that she and Jack have had a different upbringing to most teenagers their age and grew up fast. Without further argument Sharon sets a generous 12.30 a.m. curfew.

According to Sharon, the show's appeal was the very fact that despite their eccentricity, the family in many ways lived ordinary lives. 'When you usually see rock-'n'-roll families, they live the traditional, clichéd rock-'n'-roll lifestyle,' she explained. 'It sounds ridiculous to say, but we live a very normal life. I mean, we're privileged – Ozzy is a legend – but we're not at a Mick Jagger or Rod Stewart level where you've earned fortunes. We're not surrounded by huge entourages and we don't go to every opening of a sardine can. We like to spend time at home. I love going home to my kids and my dogs and sitting in bed.'

But not everyone found Sharon's behaviour amusing. Just as Ozzy's stage shows had attracted their critics in the early days, there were plenty of people ready to line up and attack Sharon for setting a bad example. Leora Lowenthal, a senior social worker at New York University Hospitals Centre, was just one of them. Partly in a reference to Jack's interview quoted earlier, she complained: 'I'm not a fan of peeing in your children's beverages. I'm also not a fan of flashing your kids' friends. It's too provocative. Teenagers are too young to understand the goofiness in that. They're just like, "Oh my God! Mom's boobs!"'

As the series unfolded viewers got to see more and more of Sharon's unique character every week. Sharon in the office dressed up to the nines, trying to decide how much to charge for a pair of Ozzy Osbourne knickers on tour; Sharon slobbing around at home first thing in the morning in her pyjamas with no make-up on. Mums everywhere warmed to her as she complained how much she hated cooking and washing-up, with a dig at America's favourite home-making guru Martha Stewart.

'Martha Stewart can lick my scrotum. Do I have a scrotum?' she remarks to the camera on one occasion. It's clear that Sharon has never been an ordinary stay-at-home cooking-and-cleaning kind of mother, for when she complains to Kelly that Ozzy's television disturbs her when she is in the kitchen preparing dinner, Kelly retorts: 'You haven't cooked for me since I was six.'

As much as Sharon enjoyed the attention, she was also delighted about the profile *The Osbournes* had given her husband. Sharon had always felt that Ozzy was one of the underdogs of rock. In recent years he hadn't been seen as particularly cool. He had never attracted fantastic reviews or hung out with the fashionable crowd. But all of a sudden things were different, and if any indication were needed as to just how far Sharon and Ozzy had come, their invitation to the White House summed it all up. Just a few years back Ozzy was considered a washed-up alcoholic rock singer and Sharon was unknown outside the relatively small world of heavy-metal music. Now no less than President Bush wanted to meet them. The occasion was the prestigious White House Press Correspondents Dinner. It was an incredible honour, particularly as the President singled out Ozzy by name in his speech. At the start of his address he introduced his guests as: 'Washington power brokers, celebrities, Hollywood stars, Ozzy Osbourne . . . OK, Ozzy might have been a mistake!' As the tables erupted in laughter and cheers Ozzy jumped up and waved, soaking up the applause. As he explained in awe afterwards: 'I thought I'd be on a Wanted poster on his wall, not invited to his place for tea.'

Sharon and Ozzy weren't only in demand with the President of the United States. Just weeks later they were invited to Buckingham Palace to attend the Queen's Golden Jubilee Concert on 3 June 2002. Sharon and Ozzy were indeed mixing in high society now. Not only did the guest list contain some of the greats of rock and pop – Sir Paul McCartney, Sir Elton

John, Rod Stewart, Tom Jones and Eric Clapton – almost every single member of the royal family would be attending, including Prince Charles and Princes William and Harry. Ozzy performed 'Paranoid', his greatest hit with Black Sabbath, and afterwards Sharon and Ozzy mingled with their royal hosts. If Sharon was daunted by such company she certainly didn't show it, laughing and joking her way through the evening.

The Queen had opted for an early night, but all the other members of the royal family were there and all of them at various points in the evening asked to meet Sharon and Ozzy, including Prince Charles and Camilla Parker Bowles. Sharon had long since been a fan of Camilla, whom she thought was a strong and dignified woman. When they were introduced, Sharon couldn't help but tell her so, exclaiming: 'I think you're fucking great!' It wasn't the usual courtly language, but it certainly got the message across. A few royal aides standing by gasped and visibly paled, but if Camilla herself was shocked by Sharon's language, she certainly didn't let it show and when Sharon started to apologize, Camilla quickly silenced her. 'Oh, it's quite alright. We curse quite a lot round here,' she replied with a smile. Worse was yet to come, however. As the two women chatted away like old friends, Sharon couldn't help but notice that Camilla was wearing a stunning and particularly low-cut gown, which revealed her ample cleavage to great effect. Without hesitating, she reached across and grabbed a hold, telling Camilla admiringly, 'You've got gorgeous tits.' Camilla, to her credit, remained composed and, rather than calling for security, took the compliment at face value and simply smiled and thanked Sharon once again.

Sharon then turned her attention to Princes William and Harry, cheekily pinching their bottoms. Even Prince Charles couldn't get away. As Sharon revealed afterwards: 'I pinched his bum and his security guard, you know, with the old earpiece in, was just cracking up. I was going around pinching him as he was talking to people. Everyone was so straight-laced. But I swore in front of them and I'm like, "Come on, let's have a party." Camilla just stood there and let me grab her tits. The princes were shocked that this mad old rocker woman was pinching their arses. Charles just sort of raised his eyebrow.'

For once it was Sharon making the headlines rather than Ozzy, and it was his turn to be shocked. 'My eyeballs nearly flew out of my head,' he admitted, after witnessing his wife's antics. If Ozzy was perhaps getting a taste of his own medicine, Sharon was revelling in her new-found status. Ten years earlier she would have been horrified by such media attention, but things had changed. Slim and dressed from head to toe in stylish designer clothes, she felt confident, assured and attractive. Where previously she had put on the tough ball-breaker act to frighten those in the music business who tried to intimidate her, she now no longer had to pretend. This was how she woke up feeling every day and she wasn't afraid to let the world know.

CHAPTER NINE

Fighting for Life

*❝ I always knew how precious and lucky it is to be alive and
now even more so. I have a million more things I'm going to do.
And I'm not going anywhere. ❞*

SHARON AND OZZY FLEW BACK to Los Angeles in June 2002
on a high after their appearance at the Queen's Jubilee
Concert. On the music front Ozzy had a new single out called
'Dreamer', which made number eighteen in the British charts.
There would be another successful and lucrative tour with
Ozzfest 2002, and in July Sharon and Ozzy planned to celebrate their twentieth wedding anniversary by renewing their
marriage vows. On top of that, this was the year when Sharon
had been named in *People* magazine's list of the fifty most beautiful people in the world. More importantly, a second series of
the hugely popular *The Osbournes* had already begun filming.

Following the success of the first series, TV executives had
begged the family for some more episodes. This time around
Sharon had driven a hard bargain and negotiated a fee of
£12 million. She had also put together a soundtrack for the
show called *The Osbourne Family Album*, featuring several

heavy-metal tracks, some of the family's favourite songs, plus a couple of Ozzy's hits and Kelly's version of 'Papa Don't Preach'. As she bluntly put it: 'You win the lottery once in your life and I'm cashing in that ticket. I'll never have an opportunity like this again to make this sort of money. Sure, Ozzy's made some unbelievable money in his life, but to get that money the work has been brutal. Touring destroys your body. So I went for it.'

At the same time she was determined to protect her brood from the darker side of fame. Several magazines and newspapers had commented on Kelly's and Jack's weight and appearance and while Sharon was happy to take the barbs about herself and Ozzy on the chin, she felt her children were too young to be made targets. In interviews she would often speak out in their defence.

When she caught two Los Angeles DJs making fun of Kelly on the radio her maternal instincts took over and her infamous quick temper kicked in. She picked up the phone and called them direct, giving them a piece of her mind and telling them to pick on someone their own size – not a teenage girl who was a novice to the fame game. She came off the phone chuckling while her family hooted with laughter around her. Sharon and Ozzy had been through some difficult times in their lives, but for once almost everything seemed to be on the up.

Their only problem seemed to be Ozzy's health again. Feeling exhausted and with a tough tour ahead of him, Ozzy decided to check himself into a local private hospital for a full physical examination. Doctors found several polyps on his colon. They weren't serious, but Ozzy was so shocked that he'd developed the growths without even knowing about it that he began to nag Sharon to have a medical too. The children joined in – they all felt their mum hadn't quite been herself of late, and finally Sharon gave in. 'I absolutely hate doctors and hospitals even

On top of the world: Sharon puts on the style at the Royal Variety Show in London in December 2004. If a sign were needed of her new iconic status, afterwards she chatted with HRH the Prince of Wales.

Above: Back in Black: Sharon and the family pose for a publicity shot for their TV show *The Osbournes* in 2002, as MTV executives hurriedly commissioned a second series. The programme is the highest-rated show in the channel's twenty-year history.

Below: Sharon plays host to the relatives she had not seen for twenty years due to her feud with her father. Pictured in LA in 2003, left to right: Sharon's cousin's daughter Sara Cowen, Sharon, her cousin Danny Somers, father Don Arden, brother David Arden and aunt Eileen Somers.

Right: Sharon with her father in Santa Monica in August 2002. The two were finally reunited the previous year after a hostile twenty years apart.

Below: You to Me Are Everything: Ozzy embraces Sharon as they arrive for the 2002 Emmy Awards in Los Angeles.

Above: Jack and Kelly Osbourne.
To Sharon's anguish, both succumbed
to drug addictions just like their father.
Kelly was admitted to a drug
rehabilitation centre in April 2004
and Jack received treatment in
April 2003, only three months
after this picture was taken.

Left: Sharon receives the devastating
news that Ozzy has been seriously
injured in a quad-bike accident at their
home in Buckinghamshire, in
December 2003.

Above: Wanted: Sharon and Ozzy appear at a police press conference to appeal for the return of priceless jewels following a robbery at their home in Chalfont, St Peter, Buckinghamshire in November 2004.

Below: Don't mess with this mother: despite the family's problems, Sharon bounced back in typically robust fashion, cheekily greeting journalists at a press conference in New York (*below left*) and having fun with old friend Sir Elton John at a fund-raising dinner (*below right*).

Above left: Sharon finally silences her *X Factor* co-judge and long-standing foe Simon Cowell in November 2004.

Above right: Give it up for Sharon Osbourne: Sharon jubilantly greets the *X Factor* audience, accompanied by one of her favourite dogs.

Left: It Asda be Sharon. *The X Factor* raised Sharon's British profile to such an extent that she was named as the new face of supermarket chain Asda in January 2005. Shoppers voted her the perfect role model for mums.

Above: Not content with mixing with the royals, Sharon met Prime Minister Tony Blair at the *Daily Mirror* Pride of Britain Awards in March 2004.

Below: Sharon with the critically acclaimed band Franz Ferdinand, as she presented them with the Band of the Year Award at a *GQ* magazine awards ceremony in September 2004. After more than thirty years in the music business, Sharon still champions emerging talent and continues to be seen as a key figure in the industry.

Above: Whatever her many and varied achievements, Sharon has always been most proud of her children. To her delight, Aimee, Kelly and Jack all turned out when, in April 2002, Ozzy was prestigiously honoured with the 2,195th star on the Hollywood Walk of Fame in Los Angeles.

Left: Sharon Osbourne in May 2003. A role model and iconic figure, her honesty, wit and charm have struck a chord with women of all ages across the world. It surely won't be long before Sharon's name joins that of Ozzy's on Hollywood's legendary Walk of Fame.

more. But to make him happy I went along for the check-up,' she recalls. Sharon was told that initial blood tests revealed she was anaemic. Fearing internal bleeding, doctors told her they wanted to investigate further. On 3 July Sharon underwent a colonoscopy, in which a flexible lighted tube is inserted to examine the lower intestine for any abnormal growths.

Thinking no more of it Sharon flew to New York the next day to catch up with her children. Jack was doing a round of media interviews, normally shy Aimee had been persuaded to do her first photo shoot for a New York magazine and Kelly had moved to the city for two months to begin work on her first album. After a successful day in the recording studio Sharon and Kelly returned to the apartment Kelly was renting, where Sharon found an urgent message on the answering machine asking her to contact the hospital immediately. She called and to her shock was told that the tests had revealed cancerous growths and that she must return immediately for surgery. Sharon and Kelly burst into tears and held on to each other for support before calling Ozzy, Aimee and Jack to break the terrible news. They flew back to Los Angeles the following day. Ozzy met them at the airport, taking one of their pet dogs along with him to cheer Sharon up. It didn't work. As soon as Sharon set eyes on Ozzy, the two fell into each other's arms in tears and hugged each other tight. That evening the Osbournes' personal family doctor received a call asking him to attend the house urgently. Fearing the worst about Sharon's health he drove straight round and rang the bell. To his surprise it was a very calm-looking Sharon who answered the door. The problem, she explained, wasn't with her own health right now, but with Ozzy's. While Sharon was succeeding in remaining remarkably strong, despite her worst fears, Ozzy was in such a state of panic that he needed sedation. 'He was hysterical, a complete wreck, just terrified,' recalls Sharon. 'I started feeling worse for him and my children than I did for myself.'

The two of them stayed awake all night just holding each other and the next day travelled to the Los Angeles Cedars-Sinai Medical Center, where Sharon underwent a four-hour operation to remove twelve inches of colon and twelve lymph nodes. Unfortunately there were complications and when the operation was over Sharon was rushed straight to intensive care, where she received a blood transfusion of three pints. But worse was yet to come. When Sharon woke up the next morning it was 4 July – her twentieth wedding anniversary – but there was no time for celebration. Two of the lymph nodes removed during the operation had tested positive for cancerous cells, which meant that the disease had spread outside her colon. By the doctors' reckoning it was stage two colon cancer, which gave her only a one-in-three chance of survival. To stand any chance of fighting it, she needed to begin an immediate three-month course of chemotherapy. Sharon typically made light of it. 'It was the most embarrassing moment, because it can only be Sharon who gets it up the bum,' she joked. 'I mean, why couldn't I have had a cute heart-shaped polyp on my vagina?' But the humour hid her very genuine fears for her future. As she admitted candidly: 'You're frightened. My stomach was in knots. I couldn't breathe. I was hysterical. And the first thing you think of is – oh my God, my kids, my kids, this can't be happening to me. You know, I'm not ready. It's not my time.'

Sharon returned home in order to gather her strength for the treatment. Doctors had told her the chemotherapy would take a lot out of her and she should prepare for it with a healthy diet full of lots of nutritious food, plenty of rest and no stress. Sharon decided to spend some weeks at the family's beachfront home in Malibu, but within days it became clear it would be business as usual. She felt she'd had time to come to terms with the diagnosis and was already feeling in a more positive frame of mind. She ordered her children to stop tip-toeing around the house for fear of disturbing her, sent Kelly back to New York to resume work on her album, and even dressed herself up and went out for a manicure and pedicure. She might have cancer, but that didn't mean she couldn't look her best.

After much thought Sharon also agreed to allow the MTV cameras back into her home to start recording the second series of *The Osbournes*. She had negotiated the deal before she was told she had cancer and, after the diagnosis, initially felt it would be best to pull out. But now she decided that the show must go on. 'We want the show to be comic. So if there is anything funny about cancer, we want to find it,' she explained. But privately Sharon had other reasons for going ahead. Her children, she thought, would realize just how sick she was if she pulled the plug on the second series and that would terrify them. Better to pretend that things weren't so bad. On Sharon's say-so Ozzy even returned to Ozzfest briefly, inviting Sharon's father Don along to one of the shows for some moral support. But it was too hard for Ozzy to concentrate on music when his wife was so ill and after a few shows he announced he would be taking a three-week break from the tour to be at her side when she began chemotherapy on 29 July. Ozzy's heart was certainly in the right place, but after just one chemotherapy session Sharon decided it would be better if she went to the hospital alone. It wasn't that she didn't appreciate Ozzy's support; it wasn't as if she didn't need it at such a bleak time in her life, but she decided it was not fair to the hospital staff, already working extremely hard. For on their very first visit Ozzy had passed out and the doctors had ended up spending more time looking after him than Sharon! Ozzy found the whole thing almost impossible to cope with. Most of his days were spent pacing up and down at home in tears, unable to comprehend the thought of a future without Sharon. As he explained: 'People say to me, "Ozzy, you've got to be strong for Sharon." And I'm no Superman, you know. Shares in Kleenex must have gone up tenfold.' Not for the first time since they met, it was Sharon who was holding the whole thing together. The family had always looked to her for inspiration, guidance and strength, and even in her darkest hour things were no different. As Sharon struggled to keep things as normal as possible at home, she decided the only thing that would help Ozzy would be for him to go back on the road. A week later – on her orders – he was on a plane heading for Clarkston, Michigan, to resume the Ozzfest tour. As Ozzy admitted: 'I was getting on Sharon's nerves.'

With her health so poor it would have been understandable for Sharon to retreat into the security of her home and cut herself off from the outside world, but that wasn't her way. Even in the midst of her own suffering she was aware that there were others in equally terrible, if not worse, situations. One of these was a young friend of Kelly's, by the name of Robert Marcato. His mother had been suffering from colon cancer and when the illness forced her to give up her job, Sharon stepped in and insisted on helping out the family financially. But that wasn't all. When Robert's mother sadly passed away in July, Sharon insisted the teenager move in with them, even giving him his own space in the guest house.

At the end of August Sharon's health took a turn for the worse and she was rushed back to hospital – this time critically ill. Between her weekly chemotherapy sessions she had been going home to recover, but each time she returned weaker. 'I had no bowel control, no nothing – it was awful,' she recalls candidly. Unable to eat, her weight plummeted and she was constantly sick. On this particular occasion her body could simply cope no more. It was Jack who found her, lying in bed, barely conscious. He immediately called an ambulance. Sharon recalls: 'I had no white blood cell count. I was totally dehydrated and I slipped into a coma and was just going under. My blood pressure is extremely low anyway and I just floored.' The ambulance sped them through the streets of LA, sirens blaring, and Sharon was rushed through the hospital corridors on a stretcher into surgery. Doctors were only able to resuscitate her with electric shock. A terrified Jack stood outside the doors not knowing if his mother was dead or alive. As he waited for the news, he frantically called Ozzy, Kelly and Aimee, who all flew straight back to be at their mother's bedside. When the doctors came out to tell Jack that Sharon had survived, he wept with relief, but it was to be eleven days before Sharon was considered well enough to leave hospital and go home again.

As soon as she did she insisted once more that Ozzy return to the tour. He did as he was told, but he found it agonizingly hard; Sharon was his soulmate and he would call her literally dozens of times a day, often in tears, to check that she was all right and tell her he loved her. On tour he told one audience as he led them in chants of Sharon's name: 'My spirit's sick. When someone you love is sick, you can't go on stage and pretend you haven't got a broken heart.'

But worse was to come. Just weeks later Ozzy received another frightened phone call from Jack, telling him that the same thing had happened all over again. Once more he had found Sharon lying in bed almost unconscious, called an ambulance and travelled to hospital with her, waiting again outside the door while doctors desperately fought to resuscitate her. 'It was the white blood cell count again and I had to be given five pints of blood,' Sharon recalls. 'I must say both times – even when I had the paddles on my chest – I wasn't scared at all. The one thing from all this is that I'm not scared of dying.'

And she genuinely wasn't. Strong and calm, she now found herself able to cope as those around her fell apart. Her inspiration was her family. She knew they needed her. She was their rock and she couldn't bear the thought of what would happen to them if she wasn't around. 'I would look in my husband's eyes and see the fear and I would think "I've got to fight, I just cannot go,"' she explained.

Of course, it wasn't easy. The chemotherapy still left her weak and she was now forced to spend much of her time in bed. It had also made her hair fall out – even her eyelashes – but Sharon refused to feel sorry for herself. Many in her position would simply want peace and quiet, but Sharon seemed to thrive on and relish the chaos around her. Every room was almost always full of people – children, friends and the Osbournes' ever-present staff. As well as a nanny to supervise the children, Sharon and Ozzy also now had their manager, a housekeeper, a chef, a cleaner, a driver and a security guard. On top of that were the dogs – there were seven now and only a couple of them anything like housetrained. The finishing touch was added by the camera crew. Two of them quit because they felt so uncomfortable and intrusive filming Sharon when she was literally throwing up in the sink. Yet none of it seemed to put Sharon off her stride. As she recalls with humour: 'I lost all my hair and the dog got the bloody wig. I was in bed dying and took the wig off and put it on the bloody table and then the dogs were running around the house chewing the wig.'

Despite her illness Sharon did everything she could to look her best, putting on her make-up and even contemplating a visit back to Dr Stevens for her regular Botox injections to remove the frown lines from her forehead. Not surprisingly the children put their foot down over that one. They had never approved of Sharon's cosmetic surgery, but as Sharon herself admitted: 'Why should they? It's very vain. It was important to me, not them.' They also pleaded with Sharon to remove her gastric band, but she refused. She was so sick that she agreed for it to be loosened in order to be able to eat more, but she was too frightened to go back into a hospital for yet more treatment, unless she really had to.

On 13 August Kelly's first single, 'Papa Don't Preach', was released in America and the following month, on 9 September, it was released in the UK, reaching number three in the charts the following week. Sharon was delighted and immensely proud of her daughter. Her only regret was that she couldn't guide Kelly through the recording of her album as she had planned. However, that didn't stop her from getting involved in her daughter's life in other ways. By now Kelly had her first serious boyfriend, Bert McCracken, the lead singer of rock band The Used. Sharon was unimpressed and, to Kelly's horror, when she met Bert for the first time she asked him directly why his nickname was 'Cauliflower Dick'. It was too much for the two youngsters, who fled from the room in embarrassment as Sharon howled with laughter. Although she had concerns about Bert, Sharon was actually delighted that her children were establishing lives of their own; something she had always hoped for. Kelly's singing career seemed to be going from strength to strength, Jack was still working as a record-company talent scout in Los Angeles and Aimee, who still lived in her own apartment around the corner from them, was busy writing her own music.

Yet as much as Sharon delighted in her children, they were growing increasingly worried about her. At times they wondered if she had even taken on board how seriously ill she actually was. Often they would wander into her bedroom and catch her on the phone making business calls – even negotiating her own television chat show for the following year. They pleaded with her to stop, telling her she already had enough money and fame to last a lifetime. To them, it was that simple. But for Sharon it was altogether more complex. Part of it stemmed from a very real fear that if she lost her will to work she would lose her will to live, but that wasn't everything. She couldn't quite explain it and she couldn't even properly understand it herself, but she needed to work. She needed to go on achieving and exploring what was out there. She was driven and she just couldn't stop.

In early September 2002 Ozzy finished his tour and came home. As Sharon quickly discovered, her health problems had taken their toll on him. He was now drinking heavily and on the verge of a nervous breakdown, needing both nursing and psychiatric help to keep him together. He was hugely support-ive on a practical level – when Sharon was too weak to walk he would carry her out of the bedroom, wash her, change her and tenderly carry her back. But mentally he found it hard to cope, preferring to sleep on a sofa in their bedroom rather than in bed with Sharon. 'He thought I wasn't going to wake up and he didn't want to lie in bed with me and wake up and find me dead,' Sharon explained candidly.

On 14 September Sharon felt well enough to make her first public appearance since being diagnosed with cancer. *The Osbournes* had won an Emmy award for 'best reality-TV series', and as one of the show's producers Sharon went along to accept it, taking Kelly with her. The cheering audience were clearly delighted to see her, but the biggest applause of the night came when she accepted the award on behalf of her husband, saying simply, 'Ozzy, I love you.' Her illness might have sent Ozzy back to the bottle and caused her endless worry, but she was still as devoted to him as ever. 'My husband is the funniest guy you could ever meet and the most honest and loving,' she explained. 'He's pulled me through.'

While Ozzy set about a detox after his recent drinking bouts, Sharon set about concentrating on being a mum again. She hadn't felt well enough to celebrate her own fiftieth birthday at the start of October, but Kelly's eighteenth birthday was on 27 October and Sharon was adamant her daughter would not miss out. She had called in party planners the previous year to ensure that Kelly had the best seventeenth birthday party that

money could buy – and amidst the canapés and pumpkin decorations there had been skeletons and contortionists. Her
eighteenth now had to surpass that. As a surprise Sharon booked
out Los Angeles' exclusive Lutece Restaurant, a regular haunt
of the rich and famous. But although the place was used to
catering to the whims of stars it had never seen anything like
this before. While the menu was conventional – prime rib,
shrimp and a two-tiered chocolate cake with pink icing trim –
Sharon had also laid on a couple of drag artists to entertain
guests, and the highlight of the evening was Sharon and Kelly
joining a male Tina Turner impersonator on stage for a raucous
rendition of the Prince song 'Star'.

Sharon's positive attitude to her illness was by now proving
an inspiration not only to Ozzy and their children, but also to
the world at large. She had publicly acknowledged that years
and years of eating junk food may have contributed to her ill
health – although doctors insisted her gastric band operation
had not increased her risk of colon cancer. But she refused to
have regrets. 'I've been through worse. I'll get through this,' she
explained simply. The truth was that rather than feel sorry for
herself, Sharon just felt glad to be alive. She had always felt that
life was a precious thing and had never taken anything for
granted. The cancer had simply made her appreciate her life even
more. She had a million and one more things she wanted to do
with it and she wasn't going to let anything stop her.

In November Sharon and the family were invited on to
American television to be interviewed by news veteran Barbara
Walters. The show attracted some of the highest viewing figures
in ABC News history as Sharon opened up about her life, illness and children. After revealing that Ozzy was taking
anti-depressants and pills for his anxiety and that her illness
had made him return to drinking, she talked movingly and
frankly about her cancer. Aimee Osbourne appeared on the

show too, giving her first ever interview and revealing how *The Osbournes* made her feel uncomfortable. What's more Sharon too revealed her own misgivings about the show, insisting that if she had her time again, she would not have done it, despite everything it had given her. She explained to Barbara Walters: 'The cameras are here all the time. So we have no privacy. You know when you're sick; you want to be on your own. And it's had a tremendous effect on Ozzy and Ozzy's been hitting the bottle again. And I can't throw up on my own and Ozzy can't get drunk on his own.' Sharon also announced that she was calling it quits when the ten-episode second series had run its course. One of the many millions watching the show that night was MTV President Van Toffler, who immediately picked up the phone and called Sharon. As far as he was aware she had committed to twenty episodes and this was the first he had heard that she had changed her mind. Shortly afterwards a contrite Sharon issued a statement via MTV confirming she would complete the remaining ten episodes as agreed. 'I love my MTV,' she said. Afterwards a relieved Toffler said that Sharon had told him, 'You know you can't believe everything I say.' He added diplomatically: 'She was probably having a difficult time and was venting in the moment. I've developed sort of an iron stomach because of Sharon Osbourne's volatility. I'm accustomed to this and perhaps the rest of the country isn't.'

CHAPTER TEN

Family Crisis

❝ *I've never been a really private person
because I've got such a big mouth.
There are no secrets.* ❞

DESPITE SHARON'S MISGIVINGS about *The Osbournes* there was no holding the show back now. Series One had taken America by storm and in November 2002 it was the turn of Britain for real – the show had already gone out on MTV but only a fraction of households with cable or satellite had been able to see it. This time round it was being screened on terrestrial television, on Channel 4. Then just three weeks later, in the States, 6.6 million viewers sat down in front of their television screens for the much-awaited launch of the second series. Things had certainly changed. There had been an innocence to the show the first time round, which couldn't be recreated; Kelly and Jack now even had their own lawyers and business managers. In a sense the second series showed what the first series had done to all their lives. Yet it was still compulsive viewing to the outside world, if not to the Osbournes themselves. Ozzy refused to watch, Kelly and Jack were never in when it was screened and Sharon had seen each episode only once, before transmission. Her own TV viewing consisted of far more escapist fare, such as *Sex and the City*, *The Sopranos*, *Law & Order* and 24.

Although the first series had attracted its fair share of criticism, a great deal of it aimed at Sharon's language, her sometimes crude antics and her lifestyle choices, she refused to change her ways for Series Two. 'You've got to be brutally honest. Otherwise it's not real and you get busted,' she explained. 'What you see is what you get. Somebody with a regular steady system in their life might consider us out of our minds. For us it works. I was brought up exactly the same way.'

As well as seeing Sharon cope with her gruelling chemotherapy treatment, viewers also witnessed her struggles to maintain order with her brood as they grew older and increasingly independent. A shocking fist-fight between Kelly and Jack ends with Jack suffering cuts to his face. In one episode Kelly comes home with a pierced nose – much to her mother's horror. On another occasion Sharon cannot hold back her tears when she discovers that Jack had her name tattooed on his back in white ink when he discovered she had cancer. All four family members made for compelling viewing. With Osbourne-mania reaching a peak Sharon sanctioned the production of a whole raft of merchandise, from model dolls to pens, piggy banks, T-shirts and mugs bearing the slogan 'The Osbournes – The Parents You Wish You Had'. A few years back Ozzy's fans would have snapped up anything with their hero's name on it, but now Kelly, Jack and especially Sharon had the same pulling power.

Everyone seemed to identify with her. Daughters wished their mums were as open and frank with them as Sharon was with Kelly; older women and mothers empathized with her and respected her honesty; others simply found her downright funny.

It wasn't so surprising then when Sharon was asked to record an Alternative Christmas Message to be shown on Channel 4 at 3 p.m. on Christmas Day – exactly the same time as the Queen's traditional Christmas message was being broadcast to the nation on BBC1. As a Channel 4 spokeswoman explained: 'Sharon Osbourne connects with our viewers in a way that the Queen can't. She is a real person who leads an extraordinary life.' And it was true. Sharon might live in Beverly Hills; she might have the best plastic surgeon money could buy and a wardrobe full of designer clothes, but as *The Osbournes* showed, none of it made her any different. She had the same problems as any other mum struggling to control two warring teenagers, she was irritated by noisy neighbours, she lost her temper and she swore, she watched television and she cleaned up after her dogs. People admired her, respected her and were fascinated by her.

When the Christmas Day broadcast went out, Sharon was seen in her own home, just like the Queen. Like the Queen she was dressed in her finest, just like the Queen she had her pet dogs around her and just like the Queen she talked glowingly about her family's achievements during the past year. Sharon for once was on her best behaviour and it was only when the credits began to roll that she allowed her wicked streak to break out. Cuddling the dogs under the tree and looking every inch the demure housewife and mother, she looked up and grinned at the cameras. 'Fucking Happy Christmas,' she yelled, before breaking out in laughter. It was the only bit of an otherwise impeccable broadcast that was cut.

Sharon and Ozzy decided to celebrate New Year's Eve by renewing the wedding vows they'd made twenty years earlier. With Sharon still weakened from the intensive chemotherapy treatment her family thought she might be happy with a quiet, low-key event. But 'quiet and low-key' was not Sharon's style.

Instead the couple would celebrate with family and friends at a lavish £500,000 party at the Beverly Hills Hotel. As usual Sharon was in charge, with Ozzy only finding out the scale of the event when the couple appeared together on *Good Morning America*. When Sharon broke the news a startled Ozzy exclaimed: 'Six hundred people? You're kidding me. Where was my consultation about this?' Sharon giggled and grinned coquettishly at her husband in the hope of winning him round. 'It's a surprise for you,' she replied. 'I'm not good at surprises,' Ozzy retorted grumpily.

The event went ahead, regardless of Ozzy's protestations, with Jack acting as best man, Aimee as maid of honour and Kelly as a flower girl. Sharon wore a beautiful cream gown and tiara, and Don walked her down the petal-strewn aisle. In a moving ceremony the couple exchanged vows they had written themselves. Their twentieth anniversary would always have been a moving occasion, after all they had endured as a couple over the years, but the fact that they'd had to postpone the event from July, because of Sharon's battle against cancer, made it all the more poignant. Many of the guests wept openly and both Sharon and Ozzy choked back the tears as she read out her vows, telling him: 'My darling Ozzy, for twenty years you have been my life partner. We have shared joys, sorrows, triumphs and tragedy and every day with you in my life is a blessing beyond my wildest dreams. Thank you for who you are, for all you have given me and for all that we will share together every day for the rest of our lives. I love you more than any words and any vows and any poetry could ever capture. I am privileged to be your wife and thank you for my babies.' In recognition of Sharon's Jewish roots the ceremony was conducted by a rabbi, Steven Rubin, who told them: 'The love that sparkles between you is without question the greatest gift life has to offer.'

As soon as the formalities were over the couple celebrated in magnificent style. Sharon liked nothing better than glamour and extravagance: six royal guards (in fact actors wearing Household Cavalry uniforms) directed guests through to the Sunset Ballroom, where performing midgets and strippers mingled with celebrity guests, including singers Justin Timberlake and Marilyn Manson. The family's assorted doctors were also there. A *Playboy* model, covered only in body paint, danced inside a giant champagne glass, while camp 1970s pop stars The Village People provided the entertainment alongside African drummers. A paperboy on an antique bike handed out copies of a specially produced newspaper containing stories about the Osbournes and their pets, while guests received goodie bags crammed with gifts from Sharon's favourite stores, including Saks Fifth Avenue and Tiffany's. At midnight a hologram talking head counted down the seconds to the bells, as Sharon and Ozzy sat on thrones on a balcony above the ballroom to receive the raucous cheers of the guests below. Finally, everyone was handed a special condom-shaped lollipop with the words 'Ozzy and Sharon's renewal of wedding vows' imprinted on the side.

As if that wasn't a grand enough way to end the year, Sharon and Ozzy received the news that the £12 million fee they had been paid for the second series of *The Osbournes*, combined with merchandising and marketing deals and Ozzy's DVD, video and record sales, had pushed their earnings for 2002 alone to £17 million. It was a phenomenal sum and a sign, if any more were needed, of just how successful Sharon had made them.

Sharon's first appointment of 2003 was at the American Music Awards in Los Angeles, which she and Ozzy had been asked to co-host. It was a live broadcast and there was consternation amongst the organizers about whether Ozzy would be able to keep the language clean enough for American television. They needn't have worried about him. It was actually Sharon who turned the air blue, introducing singer Mariah Carey with the words, 'She sings like a motherfucker, I fucking love her.' Ozzy wasn't far behind, leaving the audience in stitches as he remarked, pokerfaced, 'You can't take the fucking lady anywhere any more!'

The MTV cameras finally moved out of the Osbourne house in late January. They had shot enough footage for two series, which they would issue as Series Two and Series Two and a Half. The family celebrated the return of their privacy and Ozzy, Kelly and Jack hoped that Sharon would now slow down. But she just couldn't do it. Despite her illness, she was now in serious negotiations about hosting her own talk show. It was something she had secretly dreamed of for years, but had never really imagined would come true. Now, thanks to *The Osbournes*, she had the profile that television companies required.

On 27 January Kelly's second single, 'Shut Up', was released in the UK and the following month her debut album of the same name came out. Sharon couldn't hide her pride, but as Kelly drily pointed out: 'If I farted on a CD and handed it to her as my latest release, she'd love it.' But in reality Sharon really did have reason to be proud of her daughter. Kelly, it seemed, was coping well with her mother's illness, working hard and forging ahead with her life. It meant one less person for Sharon to worry about, for aside from her concerns about Ozzy, she was also growing increasingly anxious about her father. Don had become a frequent visitor to the house, even debuting on *The Osbournes*, but since being diagnosed with Alzheimer's his health had grown increasingly worse. Sharon had arranged twenty-four-hour care and moved him into an apartment close to her home so she could see him every day.

As far as Sharon's health was concerned, things were finally looking up. After the massive bouts of chemotherapy, new tests revealed no evidence of cancer. It was a cause for celebration, yet at the same time Sharon felt uncharacteristically anxious. In front of her children and Ozzy she still presented herself as the same cheerful, outgoing mum and wife she'd always been, but inside she was frightened, concerned that the cancer would come back. 'I'm just scared it's going to pop up somewhere else,' she admitted in one candid interview. 'Since childhood, I've always felt I needed to live for today, because I would never get old.'

Since New Year's Eve Sharon had been in dispute with a Los Angeles publicist by the name of Renee Tab. The two women first fell out following Sharon and Ozzy's vow-renewal New Year's Eve party. Renee, who worked for the International Creative Management agency, won a £9,500 diamond necklace in a raffle during the evening. Sharon later demanded she return the prize, accusing her of winning it unfairly, claiming she had gatecrashed the party. Renee said she had been invited as the guest of a friend of Jack's and refused to return it. When the two came face to face in a restaurant in April the feud spilled over and ended with them both filing battery charges against each other. Sharon accused Renee of attacking her, but Renee claimed Sharon assaulted her by spitting at her, calling her a 'Persian carpet cleaner' and 'names I can't repeat', and insisted that Sharon had been 'terrorizing and harassing' her for three months. Sharon even appeared on television the following week, showing off a bruised chin and giving her account of the extraordinary events. 'I want everybody to see the way I look, because I've got nothing to hide,' she told *Celebrity Justice*. 'I honestly thought my jaw was broken. I've got a bruise on my chin. My ears hurt. My neck hurts. My teeth have to be redone. But I'm alive. You're not going to put me down.'

Sharon's children had always come first in her life, since the day they were born. She had fought for them, protected them and loved them dearly. So it came as a devastating blow when Jack confessed to her in April 2003 that he had a serious drugs problem and could no longer cope alone. In her televised Barbara Walters interview just five months earlier, Sharon had defended her children when the veteran broadcaster suggested that some people thought their bad language and defiant attitudes were lowering the standards of acceptable behaviour. Sharon pointed out that they had a right to swear in their own home and didn't speak like that to other people. She added that not only did she not mind their bad language, but that she was probably to blame: 'I choose to use those words when I negotiate, when I deal with people. And I brought it home, unfortunately,' she admitted. But she vehemently denied that either Kelly or Jack were off the rails. 'My kids are mouthy, sure. And they're ballsy,' she conceded. 'Yeah, Jack smokes pot and you know, drinks his beer and has a giggle, but it's no more than any other sixteen-year-old is doing.'

Now those words, spoken so confidently, were to come back and haunt her. Jack's unorthodox upbringing meant he had grown up quickly – too quickly. He had actually begun drinking and smoking pot when he was thirteen years old and at fourteen he'd started taking the strong painkiller Vicodin from time to time. His evenings would often be spent in bars or clubs, with friends much older than himself, and by the time he was fifteen he was smoking pot and drinking every single day. Sharon and Ozzy had been aware of the drinking and pot use, but had absolutely no idea of the extent of it. When Sharon was diagnosed with cancer, Jack began numbing his pain with other opiate-based drugs including the highly powerful painkiller Oxycontin. Heroin-based, the drug was created for people in the last stages of cancer and had become one of the biggest street drugs in America. In addition Jack would take a host of other drugs, including Valium, Xanax, Dilaudid, Lorcet, Lortab and

Perocet. Things became so bad that he even contemplated suicide, thinking about taking a bottle of pills with the powerful liquor absinthe, while on a holiday in Europe.

Sharon was heartbroken when she realized how much her son had been suffering. When the shock sank in, she began to blame herself for not having realized earlier. Jack had shouldered a lot of the burden of her illness when Ozzy was away – he was the one who had rushed to hospital with her in an ambulance, not knowing if she would live or die. It was a lot for a young boy to cope with. He had tried to talk to her about his problems, once blurting out that he needed help as Sharon lay sick in bed; later, however, when Sharon said she would get him help, Jack managed to convince her that everything was fine and he was simply tired. Sharon firing on all cylinders would not have been brushed off with such a weak excuse, but with her health problems it was not that simple. Her illness had engulfed her and one of the side effects of her chemotherapy was that it left her more or less oblivious to what was happening from day to day. One result of this was that she didn't realize at the time the true extent of Jack's addiction.

And it wasn't just Jack who had problems. During Sharon's months of illness the family had slowly started to fall apart without her. Aimee no longer lived with them and Kelly was away working most of the time. With no school and no regular work, Jack came and went as he pleased and Ozzy had slipped back into many of his previous bad habits. With his nerves shot to pieces, he was drinking again and smoking pot, as well as taking his various prescription drugs. He often drifted through the days not really registering what was going on around him.

With Sharon back on her feet again, things were about to change. Furious that Ozzy had lapsed yet again she lost all patience with him and moved out, taking Kelly and Jack with her. They stayed away for four days in the hope that it would shock Ozzy into realizing exactly what life would be like for him if she left him for good. It worked – when she returned Ozzy was sober. But just days later Sharon discovered that Ozzy's problems were small compared to those of her son.

Out of the blue she received a phone call from one of Jack's friends, telling her that Jack was hooked on Oxycontin and was in a bad way. Sharon went straight to his room, took one of his suitcases from the wardrobe and threw it in front of him. 'You're going to rehab,' she announced firmly. Jack took one look at her, panicked and fled the house. Sharon was upset, but knew he would eventually return and vowed to be ready and waiting for him when he did. After a few days staying with friends Jack did come back. He recalls: 'I came home and just sat on my mom's bed, and I said, "I'm going to go pack my bags. I'm ready to go. And you know, I want to go – I need to go."'

In tears, Sharon and Ozzy drove Jack to the Las Encinas Hospital, a rehab centre that specialized in drug addiction and psychiatric care. Jack went through a difficult time, but after several weeks he made sufficient progress to be allowed home. Both Ozzy and Sharon were proud of him; he was only seventeen but had been mature enough to admit he had a problem that he couldn't solve alone. Yet Sharon felt totally shaken by the experience, feeling that the family's lifestyle might have been partly responsible for his downfall. As she explained: 'I thought that I wasn't a good mother, that I should have put more structure into their lives, we're too Bohemian – the whole thing. I felt I had let him down badly because I hadn't paid him too much attention and I hadn't monitored his behaviour more carefully. I let him hang out with people who were way, way too old for him. I could have stopped it, but I didn't.' An emotional Jack, however, had nothing but praise for the way his mother had handled the situation. 'I realized how much I hurt her and how much pain I put her through,' he explained humbly. 'There's not enough sorrys in the world that could fix it.'

In April came the annual publication of the *Sunday Times* Rich List, documenting the riches of Britain's wealthiest people. Having debuted in 2001 with £40 million, the Osbournes' wealth had increased to £43 million the following year and now in 2003 Sharon and Ozzy had grossed even more. The MTV deal was responsible for a lot of their fortune, as were the spin-off merchandising deals: Signature Networks had signed fifty-seven Osbourne licences in 2002 and was predicting more than £100 million in retail sales. The family had also signed a deal with publishers Simon & Schuster to work on a book of their lives, and Ozzfest 2002 had grossed more than £13 million. What's more, Ozzy's latest album had reached gold, his twenty-fourth consecutive release to achieve that status. All in all they had almost doubled their wealth to a staggering £85 million.

With Don increasingly ill, in May 2003 his sister Eileen decided to fly over from her home in Manchester to Los Angeles to see him. Eileen's son Danny and her twelve-year-old granddaughter Sara accompanied her on the trip, but aged eighty it was still a long and daunting journey for an elderly lady, so Sharon was determined to do all she could to make their stay a pleasant one. During the bitter feud with her father she had lost touch with his side of the family and it was twenty-two years since she had spoken to – let alone seen – her aunt and cousin. Yet on their arrival Sharon greeted them like old friends and insisted on footing the bill for them to stay at the plush Beverly Hills Hotel. The family stayed for five days, visiting Don twice daily, as well as catching up with Sharon and Ozzy and Sharon's brother David. It was their first meeting with Sharon's husband, but the rocker was the perfect gentleman; enquiring after Eileen's health and generously picking up the bill for their lunches and dinners. They got on so well that after two days Ozzy insisted they come round to the house for dinner. When they arrived Ozzy immediately took them on a guided tour. The family were impressed, but when they arrived at Ozzy and Sharon's bedroom they noticed the door was firmly shut. Ozzy reached for the handle, but just as he was about to open it, Eileen heard a scratching noise behind the door. 'That's not where you've locked the dogs, is it?' she asked, in a worried voice. Ozzy said it was, but that there was no problem and they would be fine with her. But Eileen's lifelong fear of dogs had not left her. 'No thanks, I'll pass on your room, Ozzy,' she said firmly and headed back down the stairs.

Sharon and Ozzy's housekeeper had prepared dinner and served it in the garden, and the family sat there for several hours, laughing and joking and catching up on old times. At the end of the meal Eileen noticed that her granddaughter Sara had gone missing, along with both Ozzy and Sharon. Curious as to their whereabouts she got up from her seat and headed indoors to find them. After searching several rooms she finally heard muffled voices coming from inside the library. She opened the door and poked her head inside to find Ozzy and Sharon painstakingly signing dozens of photographs and pieces of paper for Sara's school friends. 'You'll make a nice packet out of those,' Ozzy joked, but Sara assured him she had no intention of selling them and that they would be prized gifts for her favourite friends only.

During the stay Sharon's concerns about her father were never far from the surface. Despite her twenty-year feud with him, she was still at heart a little girl, devoted to him. Seeing him sick and growing ever more helpless by the day broke her heart. Frequently during Eileen's visit she would break down in tears, begging her aunt for advice on the best way to care for him.

On the final day of their visit, Eileen received a panicked phone call from home. Despite her age she was still working as the administrator of the Higher Crumpsall and Higher Broughton Synagogue close to her home in Prestwich, Manchester. The family were traditional Jews and as a boy Don had sung with the choir for eight years, so the place meant a lot to them. The call was from one of the other synagogue members. They had run into financial difficulties and didn't know where to turn. A worried Eileen poured out her concerns to her brother, who promptly wrote out a cheque for £10,000 without a further thought. But what Eileen hadn't anticipated was that Sharon too would feel moved enough by their plight to help. She said nothing, but less than a week after arriving back in Manchester Eileen opened the post to find a cheque from Sharon for £5,000, made out to the synagogue. Although Sharon's own life was a world away from Don's humble beginnings in Manchester, she had not forgotten her roots.

As Eileen's trip drew to a close Sharon decided to see her off in style, in the best way she knew how – with a trip to the shops. Bundling her into a car she headed straight for Rodeo Drive and the most expensive stores she could find. For Sara's nine-year-old sister Livvy back home, she bought a £300 handmade doll and a large cuddly teddy bear. And when she saw Eileen window-shopping outside a particularly exclusive bag shop, she dragged her inside and selected a stylish cream bag. Typically big-hearted, Sharon didn't want anyone to miss out. Aware that her other cousin Cathy had not been able to make the trip, she spotted a jewel-encrusted handbag in the window that would make the perfect gift for her. With no shop assistant on hand to reach the bag for her Sharon simply climbed into the window herself and pulled it out.

On the final morning before their flight home, Sharon and Ozzy visited the family at the Beverly Hills Hotel to say their goodbyes. Ozzy was dispatched to the hotel shop to buy more gifts, returning with half a dozen monogrammed white towelling dressing gowns. When Sharon counted up she worked out that her Uncle Harry back home had been left out and Ozzy was sent back again to pick up one more. Sharon had enjoyed the visit immensely and had relished the opportunity to spoil her relatives. It had made her realize how much she had missed having an extended family, and she couldn't help but reflect on the irony that it had taken Don's illness to bring them all back together again.

CHAPTER ELEVEN

Back on Top

❝ I'd hate it if people thought I was a diva.
I'd hate it, hate it, hate it. ❞

SHARON TOOK ONE LOOK at the high-cut trousers, the suntan, the neat hair and the smile bordering on a smirk and felt her hackles rise. If there was ever a man the total opposite to her beloved husband Ozzy, then it was Simon Cowell. Producers of her by now successful chat show *The Sharon Osbourne Show* had persuaded her that the *Pop Idol* judge would make an ideal guest for her controversial programme because – like Sharon – he wasn't afraid to speak his mind. But she had taken an instant dislike to his smooth style. As ever she was polished and polite during the interview, asking all the right questions, but afterwards there was no disguising how she felt. 'He struck me as a pompous, spoilt little boy,' she said frankly, imagining there would be little chance of their paths ever crossing again.

Her show, for which she received £2 million, had debuted on WB Television Network in America on 15 September 2003 and proved immediately popular. *Parkinson* it wasn't. One week Sharon was seen having Botox injections live on air and another week she chose to host the entire show from a giant bed, where interview guests, including singer Marilyn Manson's girlfriend Dita Von Teese, actress Ali Landry and a selection of *Playboy* Playmates, were invited to join her. Canadian rock band Barenaked Ladies provided the music, before stripping down to thongs and joining her in bed. All the men in the studio audience were given free pairs of pyjamas, while the women received red thongs. Said Sharon by way of explanation: 'I want to celebrate sex. Do you know why? Because I can! I think that sex is the most wonderful thing. People take it out of context and make too much of a fuss about it, but it's the most natural thing in the world.'

Sharon was understandably elated about the way life was unfolding. After years of living first in the shadow of her father and then in the shadow of her husband, she was now indisputably a star in her own right. No longer just Don's daughter or Ozzy's wife and manager, she was the host of her own prime-time US show. She had been persuaded to agree another deal with MTV for the cameras to return to film twenty more episodes of *The Osbournes*. The latest Ozzfest, which Ozzy had headlined as usual, had featured some of the biggest names in rock, including Marilyn Manson, Korn, Cradle of Filth and Disturbed. Not only that, but all her children seemed to have sorted out their lives. Jack was over his drugs problems and now considering a career in acting or TV presenting, Kelly was in Europe appearing as a support act on tour with Robbie Williams, and Aimee, according to Sharon, had begun writing for a magazine in New York. Still as independent as ever she had found her own flat and rejected all offers of help with her new career from Sharon. 'I asked her if she wanted me to manage her or give some advice but she told me to fuck off,' Sharon recalls. 'She's a stubborn one.' Sharon knew that Aimee resented the fame that *The Osbournes* had brought to the family. She had been eighteen when it began – a time when she had needed her mother. But the presence of the cameras had taken away the opportunity for the private chats and quality time she had so badly wanted. Sharon sadly knew that things had slipped between them during that period and felt regretful that she could never get that time back.

On 3 December Sharon gave Ozzy a diamond-studded Chanel watch as a present for his fifty-fifth birthday. The couple celebrated and then Ozzy caught a flight to London. He was booked up for a promotional tour of the UK to publicize 'Changes', a duet of one of his early songs that he had re-recorded with Kelly. The family then planned to spend Christmas at their home in Buckinghamshire before flying to Ireland for the New Year's Eve wedding of Ozzy's oldest son, Louis, to actress Louise Lennon. Because of their busy schedules, Sharon and the children could not fly out to Britain until later in the month, so Ozzy would initially be in England alone. On 8 December Ozzy took a day off from his tour and he and bodyguard Sam Ruston went out on their quad bikes to show a crew of MTV cameramen some new property and land he had just acquired, next door to the family's 320-acre estate. At the top of a hill Ozzy left the crew as they filmed some cattle and set off down the other side on his bike. Suddenly he ran into a pot-hole and the front of his bike buried itself in the ground. The back wheels shot up, catapulting Ozzy over the handlebars where he landed head first. His horrified bodyguard ran after him and found Ozzy face down in the mud with the bike on his back and his arm and leg twisted. When he turned him over his face had turned purple and his eyes had rolled back into his head. Sam realized that Ozzy had stopped breathing and immediately gave him mouth-to-mouth resuscitation, but when Ozzy came to he began vomiting and coughing up blood before having another seizure. Sam could feel no pulse and revived him a second time.

An ambulance was called and Ozzy was rushed to nearby Wexham Park Hospital in Slough, Berkshire, where he very quickly fell into a coma.

In Los Angeles it was 6 a.m. and Sharon was in bed when her bodyguard rushed into the room to wake her. He explained there had been a phone call from doctors in England and that Ozzy was seriously ill in hospital. In a daze Sharon haphazardly threw a few clothes into a suitcase and phoned her children. Kelly was in London recording an interview for TV's *Richard and Judy*, Jack was recording a TV show in LA and Aimee was in New York. Sharon left messages for them all before climbing aboard the first available flight, terrified that she might never see Ozzy alive again. When she arrived at his side she was horrified by what she saw. Ozzy lay there unconscious, on a ventilator, his body attached to a mass of tubes. What's more he was in grave danger of losing his left arm, due to a badly damaged artery in his shoulder. Straight away Sharon called her producers at *The Sharon Osbourne Show* to explain that she needed time off until Ozzy recovered. Heavily sedated, he was drifting in and out of consciousness while Sharon waited anxiously at his side.

The following day Sharon received reports that Simon Cowell had told Radio 5 Live that Ozzy's accident might have been a publicity stunt to help his record sales. Sharon was furious and when reporters stopped her outside the hospital a couple of days later to ask her reaction, she characteristically let rip. 'If I could tar and feather him and handcuff him to a lamp post in Piccadilly I would do it this instant,' she stormed. 'To think that anyone would stage an accident like this to get publicity is sick. You have to have a very sad mind to come up with something like this. I feel sorry for him, really, really sorry for him. I would give up my career, my fame, my money just to have my husband walk out of here with me tomorrow and I would give it all to Cowell.' The following day Simon Cowell apologized unreservedly for his comments, explaining that he had not realized how seriously ill Ozzy was. It was to be eight agonizing days before Ozzy properly came round and even then the fight back to full health would be a long one. The injuries were severe – eight broken ribs, a smashed collarbone and punctured lung, severe concussion and a crushed vertebra in his neck.

In the middle of the family's anguish, however, there was some good news. 'Changes' had given Ozzy his first number one in the British charts. It was the first thing Sharon told him as he emerged from the coma. 'He couldn't speak for tears coming out,' she said. 'It really is a dream come true for him. To me it really shows how much people love him. Because they went out and made him number one.'

Ozzy remained in intensive care until Christmas Eve when, to the consternation of the doctors, he discharged himself and returned home. Sharon was shocked by his decision, but could not be angry, such was her relief to have him back. As she admitted in a frank interview with the *Sunday Mirror* at the beginning of January 2004, she simply could not imagine life without him. So distraught was she at the very real prospect of losing him that she would have committed suicide had he died, she revealed. 'I wouldn't want to, or be able to, spend the rest of my years without Ozzy,' she explained. 'I couldn't go on without him. He is not just the love of my life, he is my life. I would have taken the coward's way out and taken pills or something.'

With Ozzy home and making a slow but steady recovery, Sharon returned to Los Angeles and went back to work. But to her shock, on her first day back she was told that her show was being cancelled following disappointing ratings. Sharon was livid. She understood that her show didn't fit the mould of other popular programmes, but was annoyed at the way it had been handled. She had called them in December to warn them she might not be able to return because of Ozzy's injuries and allegedly they had pleaded with her to come back. 'They were like, "No, we love you, we miss you. Please, you have to come back. You've got a contract. We really miss you." So I came back and the day before we started on the show, it's like, "See ya."'

Afterwards speculation was rife as to the reasons behind the decision, including suggestions that TV bosses had finally decided to pull the plug after Sharon's allegedly controversial interview with American actress Mandy Moore. Sharon had her own theories about the axing of her show, blaming the restrictions placed on daytime television in America and her predilection for asking questions that no one else would dare. 'I asked a New Zealand actor how many sheep he'd fucked,' she explained. 'I loved the show, but it was really hard. They even banned the word sausages as they said it had a sexual connotation. There is so much more freedom in the UK. Political correctness has gone mad in the United States.'

The show might have been cancelled but it had certainly paid handsomely, and in April Sharon and Ozzy featured once more in the *Sunday Times* Rich List, this time with a staggering joint wealth of £100 million. Merchandising deals were responsible for most of it, along with Ozzfest 2003, £2 million for *The Sharon Osbourne Show* and also back record sales.

After the cancellation of her show, Sharon did not have time to sit around licking her wounds. While she had been in England nursing Ozzy she had received a call out of the blue from Simon Cowell's production company, asking her if she could come along to a meeting. Intrigued, she set a date. She had not warmed to Simon at their first meeting on her chat show and his quips about Ozzy had left her incandescent with rage. But he had since apologized and Sharon was not someone to let personal differences get in the way of business. She wanted to know what Simon had in mind.

What he suggested blew her away. Following hot on the heels of the success of *Pop Idol*, he was putting together a show called *The X Factor*. It would be a similar formula, with would-be pop acts auditioning in front of three judges, but the twist would be that there would be three categories: groups, under twenty-fives and over twenty-fives. Once the judges had selected their finalists each would be awarded a category and would mentor their contestants right through to the final. Simon would be one judge and he had asked Louis Walsh, who had worked on *Pop Stars: The Rivals*, to be a second judge. For his third judge he wanted Sharon. She was delighted. Sharp as ever, she negotiated a £500,000 fee, but instinctively she sensed this particular venture had a lot more to offer than money. It would be her first stand-alone project in her home country and she was confident she had what it took to pull it off.

When Jack heard Sharon's news he was furious, telling her it was 'yellow-bellied' of her to go on a show with someone who had said so many insulting things about the Osbourne family – as well as his remarks about Ozzy, Simon had also been somewhat scathing about Kelly's talents as a singer. What's more, both Jack and Kelly felt it was too soon after her health problems for their mother to commit to such a demanding show. She had enough money never to need to work again and they wanted her to slow down. But Sharon refused. Her motivation was never simply money. It was success. And having achieved celebrity status, she was determined to make the most of every second of it.

Luckily for Sharon filming did not commence until the summer, for there were more problems at home that needed her urgent attention. All her life Sharon had had to contend with Ozzy's battle with drink and drugs. During their time together he had stayed at more than fourteen rehabilitation centres and none of them had entirely cured him of his addictions. Jack, at seventeen, had succumbed to drugs too and now, to Sharon's dismay, so had nineteen-year-old Kelly. What's more, Sharon found out about it in the most shocking way possible – via a phone call from a British tabloid newspaper. The paper had been offered photographs of Kelly taking part in what looked like a drugs deal and on 2 April contacted Sharon's publicist to ask if she wished to comment. Most celebrities at this point would have muttered a hurried 'no comment' and directed the paper to their lawyers, but not Sharon. She had always enjoyed a good relationship with the press and had generally taken the view that most publicity was good publicity. She wasn't afraid of newspaper journalists and, rare in the world of show business, she was entirely honest. If someone asked her a direct question, nine times out of ten they would get a direct answer. Sharon was in LA at the time, but asked the paper to get copies of the photographs over to her so she could assess the situation properly. She recalls: 'I saw the picture and said: "You're right, my dears, I'm sure she's doing a drugs deal." And they were like: "What?!" I said: "Print it." I wasn't gonna say she wasn't.'

She immediately told Ozzy and without further ado phoned the Promises treatment centre in Malibu, California and booked Kelly in. She and Ozzy confronted Kelly together. 'She admitted it after a lot of twisting,' Sharon recalls. 'She didn't put up a fight. It happened so quickly, she didn't have time. It was so much of a shock she said, "I'll go."' When the family's maid then revealed she had found a bag under Kelly's bed containing five hundred pills, Sharon and Ozzy realized just how serious the problem was. Sharon phoned Jack, who was at the family's beach house in Malibu, and he drove straight over to take Kelly to the treatment centre.

That night Sharon and Ozzy kept a long-standing appointment to appear on CNN's *Larry King Live* show in the States. The interview was originally planned to promote the third season of *The Osbournes*, which was to start screening in the States the following week, but instead, displaying her customary honesty, Sharon told the millions of viewers their latest devastating news. In tears, she said she could hardly believe her 'baby' had succumbed to the same problems as Ozzy and Jack. In Kelly's case her addiction was to the painkillers Vicodin and Oxycontin. 'I'm angry,' Sharon admitted. 'I'm let down. I feel like I failed again. I can't take it.' So desperate did she feel that when Larry King later asked her for advice on how to steer children away from drugs, she answered sadly: 'I'm a failure . . . how can I give anybody advice?'

With Kelly receiving treatment Sharon did some hard thinking. In her more wistful moments she regretted having moved the family to the States at such vulnerable ages, wishing she had waited until they had finished their education in England. She couldn't do anything to change the past but, she told herself firmly, there was certainly something she could do about the present. With filming of the third series of *The Osbournes* almost complete, Sharon decided that rather than commit to any more episodes she would finally call it a day. She had been thinking about it for some time, but Kelly's problems just confirmed to her that she had made the right decision. The show had turned them into international superstars and set the children up for life financially, yet Sharon felt they were now paying the price. She did not blame the cameras for Jack or Kelly's drugs habits – both children had had their insecurities and problems long before the show started – but at the same time she suspected the constant attention had not helped. They were teenagers struggling to grow up, with a mum suffering from cancer and an alcoholic dad, and the limelight had just been an added pressure on their lives. As she explained: 'It all became too much. We'd changed as a family. We'd been through so much – my cancer, Ozzy's accident, Jack's

addictions, Kelly . . . We just didn't want to do it any more
and it would have stopped being genuine. We'd become used
to the cameras. It wasn't raw or real any more. And we wanted
our home back.'

Kelly left rehab after a month and returned a changed woman.
She admitted that the four months before she had received treatment had been a terrifying time. 'I was throwing up blood and
trying to hide it because I didn't want Mum to know.' Like her
brother's, her problems had started at an early age. She had
begun experimenting with drugs at thirteen and by the age of
fifteen was taking up to fifty pills a day, but now she was better she was determined to concentrate her efforts on work,
throwing herself into the recording of a new studio album.

Feeling reassured that her daughter was on the mend, in June
Sharon flew back to London to start filming *The X Factor*. The
initial stages involved auditions that were held around Britain,
but rather than use their Buckinghamshire home as her base,
Sharon flew back to LA every time there was a break in filming.
After her family's recent problems she did not want to be away
from them for a day longer than she had to. As if more evidence
were needed of her growing status, in June Sharon topped a
magazine poll of the most important people in rock. Satan occu-
pied second place in the list, compiled by *Kerrang!* magazine,
'because the devil has all the best tunes.' The Darkness singer
Justin Hawkins made the list, but Sharon came out top for her
part in guiding the careers of Ozzy and her family. 'Sharon is
the real power behind the Prince of Darkness's throne,' *Kerrang!*
explained.

In July she and Ozzy also took time out to visit soldiers
wounded in the war in Iraq as they recovered at the Walter Reed
Army Medical Center in Washington. They spent four hours in
the hospital talking with and listening to the war stories of
dozens of soldiers, airmen and marines. Then in August the

Cedars-Sinai Medical Center in Los Angeles announced the establishment of the Sharon Osbourne Colon Cancer Program. The programme, which Sharon would front, aimed to raise money to provide sponsored care for those in need, along with specialized treatment for colon cancer patients at the hospital where Sharon herself had been cared for. Sharon was determined that all colon cancer patients should have access to the facilities and level of treatment she had received and the hospital were delighted to have her on board. As her surgeon Dr Edward Phillips explained: 'Sharon's strength, conviction and determination throughout her ordeal have inspired numerous people. She boldly allowed the public into her private world and in the process inspired us with her candour and positive outlook during a tumultuous time in her life.'

With her filming commitments in Britain it was a busy enough schedule, but not by Sharon's exacting standards. 'Now, without the camera crews, soundmen, directors and technicians roaming the house all day, the dogs are all we have left,' she joked. 'And, with our schedules this summer, it's positively quiet. But we Osbournes always have something up our sleeves.' That something turned out to be *The X Factor*. The first episode went out on ITV on Saturday 4 September and Sharon proved an immediate hit with viewers, adding a further dimension to the judging panel. While Louis tended to be the calm voice of reason and Simon revelled in his 'Mr Nasty' role, Sharon was an altogether more complex character. Capable of trading damning insults with arrogant contestants who simply wouldn't take no for an answer, she also revealed a softer side, warming to have-a-go pensioners and shedding genuine tears of her own when anyone wept and pleaded to be allowed to stay.

Predictably she livened up the proceedings by clashing with Simon in a serious of hilarious exchanges. Simon's shows had always been his babies and although people regularly argued with him, he always got the last word. In Sharon though he found he had met his match. She was not overawed by him, as many were, and wouldn't think twice about insulting him and arguing back – even tipping a glass of water over him – if she didn't agree. For Simon it proved a deeply unnerving experience. The show's presenter, Kate Thornton, explained: 'Sharon panics Simon. Winning is so important to him, yet by hiring Sharon he may well have shot himself in the foot. Sharon is absolutely his match; in fact, globally she's a bigger brand. They're both the sort of people who can pick up the phone and make things happen, but people love her because she's sincere – she cares and cries, swears and rants – and that can actually sway the way they vote. There's just a chance that the viewers might want to keep someone in the show because they like their mentor.'

In October Sharon and Ozzy hosted a fund-raising dinner, 'An Evening at Home with the Osbournes', which was attended by a host of celebrity guests, including Sir Elton John – but once *The X Factor* moved on to the final stages, which involved weekly filming, Sharon took a back seat socially and moved to their Buckinghamshire home, taking just Ozzy and Jack with her. Aimee had been settled for a long time in her own life in New York, and just before Sharon had left the States for Britain, Kelly moved out of the family home into her own apartment. It was actually the second time Kelly had bought herself a place; the first time she had invested in a £1.5 million house close to her parents' home, but in the end she decided to remain living with her family and never made the break. Having been signed up to appear in the Vancouver-based teen drama series *Life As We Know It*, however, Kelly needed to relocate. She bought a stylish loft apartment in the Canadian city and, aged twenty, began living on her own for the first time. Initially she found it hard, ringing Sharon in tears most days and leaving the television on in every room to escape the silence. But slowly she began to adapt and, having clearly inherited her mother's drive, she spent every spare second on work. As well as her acting career, she had an album in the pipeline and had also just launched her own fashion line, Stiletto Killers – a range of clothing including T-shirts, hooded tops and sweatpants, decorated with cartoons and witty slogans. Jack meanwhile had signed up to feature in a new Channel 4 show, *Extreme Celebrity Detox*, and had also agreed to take part in *The Xtra Factor* on ITV2. The show went behind the scenes of *The X Factor*, following the auditions, providing backstage gossip and interviews, and revealing what happens to the wannabes after they are shown the door.

For the final stages of the competition Sharon had been given the youngest category to oversee – the sixteen- to twenty-four-year-olds. Her mothering instinct took over immediately and she invited her five protégés back to her house for a sleepover. According to Kate Thornton, Sharon's approach was very different to that of Simon and Louis. 'She works from her head and her heart,' Kate explained. 'Sharon will say: "That little one yesterday really broke my heart." And the boys will have forgotten them already. Her tears are genuine. People have already seen her on TV as a woman, a carer, a mum and a person fighting a serious illness. But until now they haven't watched her at work. Now we're seeing exactly why she is the most powerful woman in rock. It's the one side of her that hasn't been opened up until now – and everyone adores her for it.' And her warmth didn't just extend to the contestants. While Louis took the entire production team out for a meal, Sharon invited them round to her house for dinner. Although she still had an aversion to cooking – her chef prepared the meal – it was nevertheless a big-hearted gesture. Simon, meanwhile, lived up to his reputation, pointing out the nearest Marks & Spencer and telling them to get a sandwich. According to Kate Thornton, what also set Sharon aside from the other two judges was that her show-business lifestyle genuinely seemed not to have changed her. 'She could walk into a working men's club in Aston [the Birmingham suburb where Ozzy grew up] and have everyone eating out of her hand, whereas Simon would freeze and say, "Get me out of here!"'

Sharon's two most promising acts quickly emerged as twenty-three-year-old rock guitarist Tabby Callaghan and pretty seventeen-year-old singer Cassie Compton, with Tabby the leading favourite with the bookies to win the show outright. While the other two managers maintained a friendly but strictly professional relationship with their acts, Sharon quickly became attached to Tabby and Cassie, so much so that she declared she would quit the show rather than be forced to decide between them. As she explained vehemently: 'I won't choose between my babies. No way. It's like choosing your favourite child. I'll say "fuck off" and walk out.'

With her health restored, Sharon was firing on all cylinders once more. Ozzy and the children still regularly tried to persuade her to slow down, but to no avail. Sharon was back to her old self: sleeping just five hours a night, making countless phone calls, holding business meetings and firing off idea after idea. Her latest venture was a tie-up with MTV in the States, called *Battle for Ozzfest*. Inspired by *The X Factor*, she had come up with the idea of giving eight rock bands the opportunity to battle it out on television for the chance of a tour spot on Ozzfest 2005 – the festival's tenth-anniversary tour. Each weekly episode would put the bands through a series of gruelling tests to see which one was worthy of winning the prized slot. Explained Sharon: 'Ozzfest has been the launch pad for so many new acts like System of a Down, Incubus, Slipknot, Disturbed, Godsmack and Chevelle – all who have gone on to multi-platinum success. Now we are taking eight bands and giving them the same opportunity.'

Meanwhile *The X Factor* was reaching its thrilling climax, with millions now tuning in every week, not only to watch the performers, but to revel in the banter between Sharon and Simon, which was never anything less than hilariously controversial. When Simon suggested one week that Sharon found him attractive and had visited his dressing room in her dressing gown, Sharon's reply was priceless. 'Simon said he thinks I fancy him,' she retorted. 'In fact, I'd rather have a giant lobster in my crotch than him.'

According to music commentator Rick Sky, viewers were witnessing the emergence of a different Sharon to the one who had managed Ozzy's career from the shadows for so long. 'What she did with Ozzy, she has now done with Sharon, almost,' he explains. 'She hasn't changed radically, but fame does things to people and she is much more confident and ego-driven now. When she shouts people jump – not just Ozzy.' If a sign were needed of Sharon's now iconic status it was the news, published in the *Sun* newspaper on 9 December 2004, that her famous burgundy locks were now the most sought-after celebrity hairstyle in the country. The paper reported that hairdressers across Britain were being swamped by women wanting to copy Sharon's cut. As Manchester hairdresser Peter Usher explained: 'We are now doing more than twenty Sharons a week. It's a strong, fashionable look that gives loads of confidence.' Sharon was flattered. And the news merely confirmed her worth. She had realized she was vital to the success of *The X Factor* – not just a bit-part player in Simon Cowell's show – and wasn't surprised when she was offered double her existing fee to take part in a second series. Yet surprisingly, Sharon did not sign up on the spot. She had found the mentoring aspect of the show more traumatic than she'd imagined and genuinely felt the pain of her protégés when they were voted off. While Simon and Louis treated the show more as a competition, Sharon was finding the emotional commitment to her acts draining and honestly did not know if she could cope with a second series, however high the fee.

CHAPTER TWELVE

Anything But a Quiet Life

❝ I love my life. I don't want to save it,
I want to live it. ❞

WITH OZZY WELL AND TRULY ON THE MEND, her cancer beaten and Kelly and Jack carving out successful careers for themselves following their drugs problems, Sharon assumed her family's problems were now well and truly behind them. Yet misfortune was to strike again, in the most shocking way possible. Finding *The X Factor* filming draining, Sharon had been spending most of her evenings at home, but on 22 November she and Ozzy were persuaded to spend a night in London, celebrating the birthday of Sir Elton John's partner, David Furnish, at the exclusive Ivy restaurant. After an enjoyable evening she and Ozzy had been driven back to their home in Buckinghamshire and then gone straight to bed. Sharon had been sound asleep until 4 a.m., when she woke suddenly. To her horror, when she opened her eyes the terrifying sight of Ozzy grappling in the dark with a masked raider greeted her.

Two thieves had evaded the hi-tech security alarm systems to get into the grounds, before breaking into the house, one using a ladder to climb into Sharon's first-floor dressing room at around 2 a.m. Once inside he had painstakingly worked his way around the house, coolly opening every drawer and even taking rings from the table at the side of the bed where Sharon lay sleeping. It was while he was going through the dressing-room drawers that Ozzy had woken. Needing the bathroom he had wandered in there and seen a silhouette. Initially he assumed it was their personal assistant, who often made transatlantic phone calls during the night, but when the person moved he realized to his horror that he was wearing a ski mask. Ozzy took one look at the room and saw Sharon's jewellery spread out everywhere and instantly grasped what was happening. Fired by adrenalin and without a second thought for his own safety, he dived at the intruder and grabbed him in a headlock as he tried to escape through the window. Ozzy fought to hold on and for a few seconds even contemplated breaking the man's neck to stop him getting away, but at the last minute he let go and the man dropped thirty feet to his waiting accomplice. Ozzy quickly called 999, but when the police arrived it was too late: the two men had made off with a staggering £2 million worth of irreplaceable gems.

The following morning a heartbroken Sharon spent hours going through the list of missing items with Thames Valley police. The jewellery was not insured as it hadn't been in a safe, but it wasn't the cost that upset her, it was the memories that made the pieces so precious. A tearful Sharon turned out at a packed press conference to list exactly what had been taken and to plead for the thieves to return the jewels, offering a £10,000 reward. The stolen items included a twenty-four-carat sapphire band known to Sharon as her 'survival' ring. She had bought it the day she was told she had beaten cancer. She had wanted to celebrate her survival, but at the same time had no idea how long she would live and wanted to have something special to leave her daughters. As she tearfully explained: 'Before I got sick, I'd made quite a lot of money from my American chat show. When I was lying in my hospital bed afraid I might not see another day, I wished more than anything I'd spent it on something special my girls could remember me by. That's why I went straight out and bought it. I told the girls it was my survival ring, that it was for them, that they would look at it and remember me the way I was – strong, a survivor. There was so much meaning in that ring. You can't buy that back. Nothing else is the same. Nothing can be that special, of the same moment, ever again.'

Also missing were Sharon's engagement ring and the couple's diamond-encrusted wedding bands, which Ozzy had bought to mark the couple renewing their vows two years before. The engagement ring was a ten-carat diamond that Ozzy had bought for Sharon in recognition of twenty-five years together. Said Sharon sadly: 'I waited twenty-five years for Ozzy to buy that for me. When we first met, we didn't have a bean. He bought me an engagement ring from H. Samuel. It cost £150 – a fortune to us in those days. I was happy, but he always said to me, "One day Sharon, I will buy you a ring fit for my queen." That's the ring he came home with twenty-five years later on our wedding anniversary. It meant so much. How can you replace love like that? I have still got my Ozzy, my wonderful, brave husband – but it hurts me that they took away a memory that is so special to us both.' The couple's watches – both limited-edition Franck Muller, with diamond faces – were stolen too, along with a large diamond rose ring, a string of pearls and a diamond-encrusted daisy necklace which had been a twentieth-anniversary gift from Ozzy to Sharon.

To add to their agony it was not the first time their home had been broken into, but the fourth in the past ten years. The last attempt had been back in January while Ozzy was recovering from his quad bike accident, but the raid had been intercepted by their security. After that Sharon had shipped all the couple's silver and paintings to their home in Los Angeles, where they had never been burgled, but she had not thought to send her jewellery too. Despite their heartache, though, she vowed the thieves would not drive them back to America. 'We're planning on spending our time here. This is our home,' she explained. 'I'll just have to buy a great big fucking lion and put it in the hallway to protect us.'

The night after the theft Sharon was due to appear at the Woman of the Year Awards in London. Many had expected her to pull out after her ordeal, but Sharon bravely went ahead. The burglary, as upsetting as it was, had not stopped her in her tracks. Nor did it bring an end to her feud with Simon Cowell. As the two met at the awards ceremony Simon laughed: 'It was well worth giving away the diamonds for that coverage.' While the press played up the disagreement between the couple, Sharon took Simon's comments in the jocular spirit they were intended. But she did have strong words for commentators who suggested that the couple were wealthy enough to go out and buy the jewels again. As she explained: 'Everyone has something to say about it. It's like people saying, "Why have they got all that jewellery?" But I've worked hard and I've come from nothing to where I am today. It's my life and at fifty-two I think I deserve all the nice things I've got and I've earned the right to spend the money I've worked hard for.'

Away from the cameras, both Simon and Louis Walsh had rallied to Sharon's aid. Simon had sent flowers immediately and arranged to meet up with her, and Louis provided a shoulder to cry on. For few people knew just how upset Sharon was by the experience, even preferring to stay in a hotel for several days, rather than return home. As Louis explained: 'It's been a shock to the system for Sharon, it's definitely affected her. Although she's slowly coming to terms with the loss of her jewellery, it's the invasion of her privacy that has left her shaken.' Sharon dealt with it in her usual way, by throwing herself back into work, spending fourteen hours a day coaching and coaxing her remaining *X Factor* contestant, young Irish singer Tabby (Cassie had left the show on 20 November, after losing both the viewers' and judges' votes). Nor had her ordeal made her nervous about being seen out and about in her jewels. Throughout the series she had constantly lent jewellery to presenter Kate Thornton, even setting aside an expensive pair of Van Cleef & Arpels earrings for her for the night of the final. As an impressed Kate noted afterwards: 'More than my house is worth!'

To Sharon's utter disappointment, Tabby was voted off the show on 4 December, so when the final was aired a week later, Sharon had no contestants left. In theory it meant she should have been impartial, but it was clear from the start which way she would be voting. She had never hidden her dislike of Simon Cowell's older solo singer Steve Brookstein, and when she was asked for her opinion after his performance of 'Against All Odds' she let rip. 'Listen, everybody knows the way I feel about Steve,' she told host Kate Thornton. 'I've never been a Steve fan. Steve has a very nice voice, for me he's not a superstar. And I just have to say this: I'm so fed up of Mr Humble and Mr "Should I sell my Volkswagen, should I keep it?" He's over-confident; he's been over-confident from day one. He's not what he seems, believe me. All that BS that he gives out every week. He's even fooled Simon! He's full of crap and he's an average singer, ask everybody else on this contest, he's overly confident. The public should know he's a fake!'

The outburst was extraordinary and shocking even by the tough standards of the competition. The judges – particularly Simon and Sharon – were known for their direct and honest opinions, but this was something else. Steve looked stunned; Simon shook his head first in surprise and then annoyance and the audience gasped in disbelief. Had Sharon just gone too far this time? Simon clearly thought so, although he managed to remain calm. 'It's inappropriate to be personal tonight,' he told her. When the results of the vote came in later it seemed as if the public had agreed with him, with Steve – to many people's surprise – beating opera group G4 to the prize. For many commentators Sharon's comments had been the deciding factor, resulting in a swing of sympathy votes for the thirty-five-year-old soul singer. But Sharon did not stay around to debate the outcome. According to newspaper reports, such was her fury that she stormed out of her dressing room still in her dressing gown to be driven straight home.

The following day it was Sharon, rather than Steve, making the headlines. More than three hundred viewers phoned in to complain about her withering attack and it quickly emerged that Sharon and Steve had already clashed in a heated row earlier in the day, during rehearsals before the show had even begun. As Sharon herself admitted: 'I just lost it with him. It got down to the level of *Jerry Springer*, it was awful. We were screaming at each other and I allowed him to wind me up.'

A furious Simon immediately declared that Sharon's future with the show hung in the balance. A second series was due to start filming in the summer of 2005 and he had already started negotiating with her and Louis. But in a press statement the next day he admitted that the latest developments might well change things. 'We did receive a record number of complaints about Sharon and as a result her future on *The X Factor* is undecided,' he explained. 'Sharon didn't do herself any favours. Her comments were totally inappropriate.'

Undeterred, the following Tuesday Sharon appeared at the Royal Variety Performance at the London Coliseum in the presence of the Prince of Wales. Ozzy had been due to be there with her, but the show had clashed with an operation to adjust a metal plate inserted in his shoulder after his quad bike crash, which had been damaged during his struggle with the burglar at their house. Instead Sharon appeared alone, alongside a host of stars, including Shane Richie, Sir Cliff Richard, Brian McFadden and Sir Elton John. Afterwards Sharon chatted backstage with Prince Charles, who enquired with great concern as to Ozzy's health and their break-in. That night Sharon also made a personal appeal on BBC1's *Crimewatch* in a pre-recorded interview, in a bid to track down the raiders who had stolen her jewels. As replicas of the stolen items were shown Sharon told the viewers: 'I'm angry and scared. I hope this will spur somebody on to say something. Tell the truth. Turn him in.'

Back at home though Sharon had other things on her mind, and she was still smarting over the *X Factor* feud. Initially she was unrepentant. The following week she gave an interview to the *Daily Mail* insisting her outburst was nothing compared to what she could have said. But at the same time she admitted that she had spent the days after the show running over and over the confrontation – to such an extent that she had driven Ozzy mad. 'Am I the biggest bitch in Britain? I've thought about nothing else all week,' she confessed. But that wasn't all Sharon revealed in the interview, for she finally admitted publicly that the bulimia which had plagued her all her life had still not gone away. 'It's a mental problem,' she explained. 'Some people turn to drugs or drink; mine was food. If I'm under stress, I hit the biscuits, crisps and the bread. The food is piled up to my throat. Then I have to go and be sick.' She admitted that her children found it upsetting and that she had promised Jack she would get help for the problem.

On 22 December Sharon appeared at the British Comedy Awards to present one of them. Organizers, worried about the possibility of another clash between Sharon and Simon Cowell, had given them dressing rooms at opposite ends of the building.

But that wasn't all; bodyguards had been hired too. As the show's executive producer Michael Hurll explained: 'We were worried that the tension has been rising since the *X Factor* final and, with the whole Osbourne family in tow, we felt extra security may be needed for the night.' But instead of looking for further trouble, Sharon surprised everyone by taking the opportunity to apologize publicly to Simon for calling Steve fake. Now she had calmed down she realized she had seriously jeopardized her chances of being invited back for a second series, which was the last thing she wanted. Accompanied by her children, including twenty-one-year-old Aimee, she was on her best behaviour, announcing contritely: 'I realized it was unfair as millions voted for him. Simon was furious afterwards. But I'd love to do another series if he'll have me and the money's right.'

Just before Christmas Sharon booked herself in for a course of Freudian therapy: one-hour sessions three times a week. She was fulfilling her earlier promise to Jack that she would seek help for her bulimia, but she had other concerns too. Her eating and her weight were permanent worries, but she was also anxious about her over-spending and her constant guilt. Ever since the children were born Sharon had tortured herself with the thought that she could have been a better mother. When she had been away working with Ozzy when the children were young, she had felt guilty for not being at home with them, and she had blamed herself for Kelly and Jack's recent drugs problems. As she candidly admitted: 'When I wake up in the morning, I think, "God, I should have been with this one, I should have been with that one." And it is this constant guilt that grows and grows.'

For Christmas Sharon and Ozzy flew the family chef out from Los Angeles to Buckinghamshire to cook a traditional festive lunch for them. As usual they were joined by their best friends, singer and record producer Colin Newman and his wife Metta –

who had been spending Christmas with the Osbournes for the past twenty-four years – and their five children. After the disappointments of her Christmases as a child, Sharon liked to make as much as she could of the festive season, dressing up in an evening gown on the day and insisting that the rest of the family follow her example, with Ozzy and Jack in suits. In the morning the family attended the local church service, before returning home to a banquet fit for royalty. As a result of her gastric-banding operation Sharon was only able to nibble, rather than tuck in to a huge plateful, but the rest of the family more than made up for it, enjoying turkey and all the trimmings. The only difference from previous years was in the traditional Christmas booze-up. With Jack, Kelly and Ozzy not drinking at all, Sharon and Aimee both chose not to touch a drop either, but that didn't stop the family partaking in the traditional game of charades . . . or the traditional row. As Sharon remarked philosophically: 'When isn't there a row at Christmas? There's always an argument. Now I just sit there and let it happen, because there's nothing you can do. It's like, "Oh, here we go, Merry Fucking Christmas."'

The house meanwhile had been decorated to Sharon's exacting standards. And while that included huge trees decked out stylishly in silver and red, it also meant the same box of Christmas decorations that she and Ozzy had put together before they even married. These had always meant a lot to Sharon, but this year, after the break-in, Sharon took particular comfort in their familiarity and the memories they evoked. While playing her favourite Christmas music – Frank Sinatra, Dean Martin, John Lennon and Slade – she excitedly unpacked the box, uncovering tiny Santas and gingerbread people, and paper decorations that the children had made in school. Sharon's present to Ozzy this year was probably her most unusual ever. Normally she liked to give him jewellery or gadgets, but for a change she had bought a £5,000 herd of twelve Japanese sika deer, which she'd had driven down from Worcestershire and smuggled onto their estate late on Christmas Eve.

Career-wise, Sharon's year ended on a triple high note. Firstly came the announcement that she was replacing popular comedienne Julie Walters as the new face of Asda supermarkets. She was chosen after shoppers voted her the perfect role model for mums. As a source explained: 'Asda liked the fact Sharon is a successful and attractive older woman. She also has a reputation as a tough negotiator who doesn't like to be ripped off. She's a good advert for the brand because people looking for a bargain can relate to her.' Secondly, she was crowned Virgin Radio's Rock Personality of the Year, beating such respected names as Sir Bob Geldof and Sir Elton John. More than six thousand listeners voted in the poll, which Ozzy had won the previous year. Explaining Sharon's success, Virgin presenter Ben Jones said, 'Sharon took on Simon Cowell at his own game and showed him who the boss was. She is a role model for the nation. Speak your mind and say what's what.' Thirdly, on a new list of the richest women in Britain, Sharon appeared at number twenty-nine, with personal earnings of £4.5 million from 2004 alone.

On Boxing Day the world woke up to the dreadful news that thousands upon thousands had perished in South-East Asia after a giant tidal wave engulfed miles of coastline. When Sharon turned on the television the following day she could hardly believe the pictures of death and destruction. She had planned a family holiday to Thailand for New Year and had been due to fly out just three days later. She knew that they had been fortunate, but that many thousands of others had not been so lucky. Immediately, she pledged to do everything she could to help. The following day Sharon read that the *Daily Mail*, like most British newspapers, was organizing a Flood Aid appeal and asking readers to send in donations, however big or small. Sharon picked up the phone and called the donation line pledging £25,000. She then called the national Disasters Emergency Committee to see if there was anything else she and Ozzy could do to help. The committee was well aware of Sharon and Ozzy's popularity and thanked them for their offer. They were about to record a television appeal to run on MTV and wondered if the couple would be prepared to front it for them. Sharon said they would be honoured.

Meanwhile, as the death toll rose in South-East Asia, Sharon's heartache grew. She and her family had been through some terrible times in the past couple of years, but nothing compared to this. She, Ozzy and the children had earned £20 million between them the previous year and, deciding that she had not been generous enough, Sharon picked up the phone to the *Daily Mail* again and pledged a further £75,000. As she explained: 'There are really no words to describe how devastated we are to see this unfold and we wanted to give some more money. We would only be spending the money on unimportant things anyway – there's no point wasting sums like that on trivial things like jewellery or clothes. It's much better being spent on helping the people in Asia.'

Now they were spending so much of their time in Britain, Sharon and Ozzy decided to put their Beverly Hills home up for sale. The house had many happy memories for them, but it was time to start a new chapter of their lives in a smaller home. The children had now all spread their wings – Jack, nineteen, was looking for a home of his own and Kelly, twenty, had her stylish apartment in Canada. For some time twenty-one-year-old Aimee had been living in New York. It was unlikely they would all live together as a family again and all Sharon and Ozzy really needed now was a decent-sized garden for the dogs.

On 17 January the final series of *The Osbournes* premiered on MTV in the States. The series picked up where the previous one had left off and covered Sharon's recovery from cancer, Ozzy's quad bike accident and Jack's rehab treatment. As the family were now going their separate ways, it was a natural time for the series to end. But there was no doubting the permanent impact it had made; not only on the Osbournes themselves, but also on television audiences and reality television. 'With *The Osbournes* we literally created a new format for television,' explained Brian Graden, President of Entertainment, MTV Networks Music Group. 'The Osbournes were the first celebrities to let the cameras into their home to film their day-to-day lives as [they] happened. The show has had an indelible impact on the larger television landscape and its success is due to the overwhelming personalities of the first family of rock 'n' roll.' Although Sharon still had her doubts about her decision to take part, she was magnanimous as the series came to a close. 'After three years, the MTV cameras became part of the family, documenting what is possibly the most dramatic year we have had,' she said. 'Though it was rough sometimes, we are truly blessed to have had this amazing experience.'

Sharon had planned to spend the early part of 2005 overseeing the March release of the *Prince of Darkness* four-disc box set, featuring highlights from Ozzy's twenty-five-year solo career. Featuring old hits, it also included a CD of covers of some of his favourite songs. But before then there was plenty of other work to be done. At the end of January Sharon and Ozzy both took part in Radio Aid – a twelve-hour broadcast featuring a host of top names, including the British Prime Minister, Mick Jagger, Chris Evans, Davina McCall and Ricky Gervais – designed to raise £3 million for victims of the tsunami. The following day Sharon appeared before the British press as the new face of Asda. As part of a £7 million campaign it was announced that Sharon would take part in the supermarket's 'Mums In A Million' TV advertisements, visiting a local store, testing the produce and talking to staff to check out whether Asda was up to scratch for modern mothers, particularly those trying to help their children eat more healthily.

As she posed for the cameras with bananas and bunches of spring onions, Sharon took the opportunity to drop her latest bombshell news: she planned to stand as an MP and launch a political career. She was in the middle of writing a new reality-TV series, she revealed, which would follow her while she ran for a place in Parliament, standing as an independent candidate in one of the London boroughs. She admitted she was supposed to be keeping it secret, but couldn't resist sharing her news and said she really hoped she would be able to help Londoners rather than do the job for selfish reasons. 'I shouldn't really tell you about it, but I will anyway,' she said engagingly to reporters. 'I am very excited about it because it is something so different. The majority of people do it for themselves, to enhance their egos. To them it is about the perks of the job and little more.'

Meanwhile Sharon was determined to continue to do all she could for the survivors of the tsunami, and two days later she was in the studio overseeing the recording sessions for a fund-raising charity record. Since she had come up with the idea, less than a month ago, she had signed up a host of stars, including Elton John, Robbie Williams, Rod Stewart, Phil Collins, Ozzy and Kelly, and Pink. They would record a cover version of Eric Clapton's 'Tears in Heaven', the moving song he wrote following the tragic death of his four-year-old son, Conor. Sharon having patched up her differences with Simon Cowell, who agreed to co-produce the track with her, the sessions began. Elton John, Velvet Revolver and Italian opera star Andrea Bocelli kicked off proceedings at London's Whitfield Street Studios. The New York recordings, featuring Rod Stewart and Robbie Williams, had to be axed when a snowstorm hit the city, so Sharon set about trying to rearrange the session at the family's own recording studios in Los Angeles, where they would sing alongside Ozzy and Kelly, Gwen Stefani and Josh Groban.

Such was Sharon's growing status that rarely a day passed when she was not featured in one of the national newspapers. The *Daily Mail* in particular, not a paper that would normally warm to such an outspoken and controversial figure, had sensed how popular she was and had now taken to using Sharon to front its Flood Aid Appeal, often placing large photographs of her on the front page. Elsewhere there were no signs of things slowing up. There were rumours that she was considering taking over and managing the career of Liza Minelli, and ITV bosses had approached her to see if she would be interested in hosting her own ITV1 teatime chat show. It would be an occasional slot on alternate days to *Des & Mel* and *Paul O'Grady* and would compete against the popular *Richard and Judy* show on Channel 4.

Meanwhile she was still awaiting a decision over *X Factor 2*. There had been intense media speculation for weeks as to whether Simon Cowell would be able to forgive and forget Sharon's outburst at the end of the previous series. Everyone knew he planned a second series to screen in August 2005, but what people didn't know was whether Sharon would be a part of it. On 29 January, the wait was over. Following a series of meetings between the pair Sharon signed on the dotted line to join Simon and Louis Walsh on the judging panel. Simon had initially been frosty with Sharon, but had accepted her apology. What's more, he knew she was a big hit with the viewers. It was worth pulling out all the stops to sign her again.

At the beginning of February 2005 Sharon flew to New York. She had agreed to take part in a tsunami relief benefit concert in the city, but prior to that she had an important date . . . with yet another cosmetic surgeon for her latest round of Botox injections. Since discovering them a few years previously, Sharon was a convert and firmly believed they were one of cosmetic surgery's greatest innovations. 'There's no recuperation, it doesn't hurt. You literally go in, have it done and out!' she explained delightedly. In addition Sharon splashed out another £30,000 on cosmetic surgery; this time enduring fourteen hours of treatment for new porcelain veneers on her teeth, courtesy of top LA orthodontist Dr William Dorfman. On this particular occasion Sharon had good reason to want to look her best, for she had been signed up to host Sky Television's Oscars night coverage live from Los Angeles on 27 February.

Furthermore, in April she was due to make her debut on London's West End stage, taking part in the controversial show *The Vagina Monologues*. A comedy, the play featured three women talking about their most intimate thoughts and experiences, and producers felt Sharon would be ideal for one of the roles. She had already proved she could act the previous year, with cameo appearances in the US TV sitcom *Will & Grace* and the American daytime soap *Days of Our Lives*. Now was her chance to do it for real with a six-week West End run. When that finished she would start filming the audition stages of *X Factor 2* and in the summer there was the tenth-anniversary Ozzfest. There was also talk of an evening-slot ITV1 chat show, jointly hosted by Sharon and Ozzy, to be screened in 2006, featuring such big-name guests as Robbie Williams and Sir Elton John. Naturally, initial planning placed the show in a post-10 p.m. slot to avoid any problems with bad language and swearing.

Not that it was Sharon's style, but had she stopped to reflect on her incredible success she could have been justifiably proud of where she now found herself. She had made her peace with her father, who was receiving the best possible nursing care in Los Angeles. And her children all finally seemed to be making a success of their lives. Jack's show *Extreme Celebrity Detox* aired on Channel 4 in February 2005, and showed him in Slovenia with other celebrities on a self-improvement course that involved mountaineering, climbing, meditation and dieting. He had found the whole experience so inspiring that he had lost some weight, given up smoking and become a fanatical climber in his spare time. In April he was due to present ITV's *Celebrity Wrestling*, but he was also now thinking about a change of career and had plans to become a New York firefighter. Kelly was still busy putting the finishing touches to her new album, which was scheduled for release in June. There was talk of a possible second series of *Life As We Know It*, which was now being screened in Britain, and she had also been offered the lead in the Broadway show *Hairspray*. Aimee, meanwhile, had surprised them all by landing herself a record deal, launching herself as a soul singer with no help whatsoever from her family. What's more, she now felt ready to join her mother in the limelight, agreeing to join her on stage in *The Vagina Monologues*. Says Sharon: 'I'm so proud of her. It's taken time for her to grow comfortable with it. She's now at the stage where she is ready to come out as Aimee.'

As for the future, Sharon keeps an open mind. Both she and Ozzy would love grandchildren, and she openly admits that if her figure and face started sagging: 'I'd have the whole fucking lot lifted again!' She is clearly happier in her skin than she ever was at twenty-five and has no regrets about the passing of time. She has her beloved Ozzy – her soulmate – a confidence and figure she could only have dreamt of as a young woman, and a career that could take her absolutely anywhere she wished – management, television, production, film or even politics. The path she chooses remains to be seen, but what is certain is that it will not be dull. She has lived fifty-two lives in her fifty-two years and has no intention of slowing down now. As Sharon herself says: 'I've been doing things for other people my entire life – for my dad, for Ozzy, for the children. Now my husband is secure with himself and his career and the children are young adults. Now it's Sharon time, it's time to make me happy.' After the life she has led, who could begrudge her that?

Recommended Reading/Viewing

BOOKS

ARDEN, DON with WALL, MICK
Mr Big – Ozzy, Sharon and My Life as the Godfather of Rock (Robson Books, 2004)

CRAWFORD, SUE
Ozzy Unauthorized (Michael O'Mara Books, 2002)

KATZ, DAVID and ROBIN, MICHAEL
The Osbournes (Andrews McMeel Publishing, 2002)

KAVANAGH, BRUCE
The Osbournes: Talking (Omnibus Press, 2004)

OSBOURNE, OZZY and SHARON, with GOLD, TODD
Ordinary People – Our Story (Pocket Books, 2003)

TUCKER, REED
The Osbournes Unauthorized (Boxtree Books, 2002)

DVDs

Don't Blame Me: The Tales of Ozzy Osbourne
(Epic Music Video, 2000)

Mr and Mrs Osbourne – Happy Ever After
(IMC Vision, 2002)

The Osbournes: Series One
(Buena Vista Home Entertainment, 2003)

The Osbournes: The Second Series
(Buena Vista Home Entertainment, 2004)

The Osbournes: Two and a Half
(Miramax Home Entertainment, 2004)

INDEX